Not for Ourselves Alone

Not for Ourselves Alone

Theological Essays on Relationship

Burton D. Carley and Laurel Hallman, Editors

Skinner House Books
Boston

Published by Skinner House Books, an imprint of the Unitarian Universalist Association, a liberal religious organization with more than 1,000 congregations in the U.S. and Canada. 24 Farnsworth St., Boston, MA 02210-1409.

www.skinnerhouse.org

Printed in the United States

Cover and text design by Suzanne Morgan

print ISBN: 978-1-55896-731-1
eBook ISBN: 978-1-55896-732-8

6 5 4 3 2 1
17 16 15 14

Library of Congress Cataloging-in-Publication Data

Not for ourselves alone : theological essays on relationship / Burton Carley and Laurel Hallman, editors.
      pages cm
   Includes bibliographical references.
   ISBN 978-1-55896-731-1 (pbk. : alk. paper)—ISBN 978-1-55896-732-8 (ebook)
   1. Spiritual life—Unitarian Universalist Association. 2. Spiritual life—Unitarian Universalist churches. 3. Interpersonal relations—Religious aspects—Unitarian Universalist Association. 4. Interpersonal relations—Religious aspects—Unitarian Universalist churches. I. Carley, Burton, editor of compilation.
   BX9855.N68 2014
   248.4'891—dc23
                                                                2013045738

We gratefully acknowledge permission to reprint an adaptation of a discernment group experience by Rose Mary Dougherty, used by permission of author; reflections about "Whose Am I?" by Victoria Safford, used by permission of author; an adaptation of "Dance of Privilege" by Mark Hicks, used by permission of author; an excerpt from "Choose to Bless the World" by Rebecca Parker, used by permission of author; an adaptation of "Good Samaritan" from *Cotton Patch Parables of Liberation* by Clarence Jordan copyright © 1976 by Clarence Jordan, used by permission of Wipf and Stock Publishers, www.wipfandstock.com; "A Walk" from *Selected Poems of Rainer Maria Rilke, A Translation from the German and Commentary* by Robert Bly, copyright © 1981 by Robert Bly, reprinted by permission of HarperCollins Publishers.

CONTENTS

Introduction

This book is about moving deeper into the spiritual practice of our faith.

Our non-creedal way of being religious as Unitarian Universalists empowers a self-reliant individualism. We often express this independence as a freedom *from* rather than a freedom *to*.

We also highly value theological diversity. While this is an essential element of our congregational way, it also makes us shy about sharing matters of the spirit out of concern for discovering disagreement. Because of our independence and diversity, we tend to become individually isolated in a spiritual bubble.

We need to break out of our spiritual *don't ask don't tell* culture in our congregational life. This book is part of a movement toward less polemic and more intimate relationships, and conversations focused on the life of the spirit rather than ideological abstractions. It invites us to be more vulnerable with one another so we can express things not easily defined in precise ways. It represents an expression of the need to grow our souls through relationship.

The hunger to be present to each other in deeper and more vulnerable ways for spiritual development is joined by a second desire to move beyond the age-old theological conundrum of giving definition to who we are as Unitarian Universalists. This question suffers from elevator speech fatigue. Collectively, we can deepen our connections by shifting the query from "Who are we?" to "Whose are we?" The transition in emphasis suggests that we are part of something larger, something that both includes us and transcends us.

"Whose are we?" is a relational question. To whom and/or what am I committed? How am I accountable? It shifts the focus from defining our identity to maturing our faith in relationship with each other and with the Holy. As the editors, we hope that these essays and related activities may serve as a plow to break the ground and create fertile ways to grow in the life of the spirit with each other.

In order to experience the core of this book, we invite you to ask at least one other person to walk through it with you. We encourage you to have a practice partner who would agree or even covenant to participate with you in the exercises found at the end of each section. If you can gather a small group of interested pilgrims, perhaps to meet monthly, all the better. Use the questions after each section for dyads, groups of four, and whole group responses. If you meet once a month the twelve essays will carry you through a year together.

Following the last section, you will find a description of a discernment group. We hope you will consider forming one as a real option, either as a next step following the work with these essays or as a way to be together as you explore the possibilities in these pages.

These exercises may involve you using language and practices that you have never tried. You may need to dust off old language to use in this new context or to infuse old language with new meaning. You may already be comfortable with using metaphors as a vehicle that allows the mind and heart to converse. Whatever your relationship to the language and practices outlined in these essays, we invite you to fully embrace them for the time you are engaged with them.

The essayists—ministers and lay members of UU congregations—have been encouraged to write from a place of vulnerability. We hope that you will meet them there.

Burton D. Carley and Laurel Hallman
August 2013

ONE

Whose Am I?

Douglas Steere, a Quaker teacher, says that the ancient question, "What am I?" inevitably leads to a deeper one, "Whose am I?"—because there is no identity outside of relationships. You can't be a person by yourself. To ask, "Whose am I?" is to extend the questions far beyond the little self-absorbed self and wonder: Who needs you? Who loves you? To whom are you accountable? To whom do you answer? Whose life is altered by your choices? With whose life, whose lives, is your own all bound up, inextricably, in obvious or invisible ways?

—Victoria Safford

Introduction

It is not possible to be a person by yourself. These essays bear witness to the power of our relationships, how they shape us and bless us. Our understanding of these relationships starts with our most basic sense of who we are by recognizing what lays claim to our hearts and lives. Who or what claims our hours and days? We not only need to name our commitments but also to have them acknowledged as essential to our lives. Blessings confirm the reality and significance of whose we are.

You Get Going and Live Like That!

SARAH LAMMERT

I'd been on the road for about five hours when we turned onto the Massachusetts Turnpike, heading east and home. It had been a fun but tiring overnight visit to a college in Pennsylvania with my daughter, a senior in high school, who was trying to decide where her future would take her. The traffic was daunting, and I was wishing we could beam ourselves home, when I saw a highway sign blinking the message "We are One Boston. Thank you all." Suddenly the traffic transformed from an annoying obstacle into a moving stream of humanity. These were my people. And, although we crawled most of the way, it seemed that in no time we arrived safely at home.

It had been a week. On Monday, the Boston Marathon was interrupted by a bombing, and nearly two hundred people were harmed; three killed. Just about everyone in Boston knew some-one running or watching the race, and we all scrambled to find out if our loved ones were okay. On Wednesday, a rabbi friend from out of town called and asked if I would pick up his marathon medal for him, as he had been stopped less than a half a mile from the finish and would not be able to return. As I walked through the thick of the impacted area downtown, the medal clutched in my hand, I stopped at the makeshift memorial at Newbury and Berkeley Streets. A pair of Buddhist monks sat in meditation at the site as people knelt around them to add flowers or take a photo, or to say a silent prayer. I found myself in tears, one of the gathering crowd. On Thursday I discovered that two elderly founding members of the church in California that had ordained me almost twenty years earlier had been stabbed to death in their homes. It began to seem as though random and brutal violence was everywhere, stealing good lives and a sense of order and safety. On Friday the city of Boston was locked down as a massive manhunt led up to the capture of one of the bombers.

So I had been happy to escape to Pennsylvania on Saturday, but my heart was still shattered and open, as grieving hearts often are, filled with both the pain and deep joy of our interconnection. For we belong to one another, irrevocably. We belong to the ones so broken by fear and alienation that they strike out without conscience. We belong to the ones in harm's way and to those who love them. We belong to the bystanders, the first responders, the runners, and the meditators. We belong to the angry, the compassionate, the confused, and those who don't seem to notice much of anything. We belong to the young and old, the able and challenged, the immigrant and the aboriginal. We belong to the breezy sunny day, the rocks and rivers, the moving earth, and the squirrels in the trees. We belong to the smokestacks and the trash and the scarred remains of explosions. We belong to a Love greater than fear and to a Power beyond the sum of our parts. We are not ourselves alone.

In 1985 I met a Maasai warrior while studying in Kenya with the School for International Living. We were building bricks for a local schoolhouse in a remote area when I and other students got invited to a dinner of fire-roasted meat with the local warriors, most of whom were younger than my twenty-one years. Yet they seemed ancient in spirit—calm and wise. In conversation, one of the young men asked me who my people were. I stumbled with my answer, explaining that I came from the area of the Mississippi River. He seemed puzzled that I could not clearly identify myself with a tribe. "I know who I am," he said gravely. By this, he meant, "I know who I am in community. I know who I am as a part of the natural world. I know myself to be a member of one tribal body. I belong; therefore I am."

This simple interchange deeply affected me. I came away from that experience feeling the profound loneliness of growing up in a culture in which individualism is not only championed, but idolized. I felt determined to find my own sense of belonging. I would eventually find it in the Unitarian Universalist Church. Unitarian Universalist values begin by claiming the worth and dignity of every individual person and allowing the complete freedom to each person to explore his or her beliefs. But countering this independent streak is a commitment to understanding oneself as a part of the interconnected web of life. In this sense, Unitarian Universalism gave me a place to make myself whole by becoming a part of something greater than just me.

We are all defined by our network of relationships: mother, daughter, son, father, friend, teacher, student, co-worker, competitor, teammate, neighbor, spouse. Obituaries sum up our lives by noting the people and places we were connected to most closely. It's clear that none of us enter (and rarely exit) the world alone, but in the United States it seems that people are getting lonelier. Sociologists like Robert Putnam, author of *Bowling Alone* and *American Grace,* have documented drastic declines in neighborly socializing, friendships, participation in groups and clubs, and even family dinners over the past twenty-five years. More and more Americans are living alone—some 40 percent in major cities and 28 percent overall, which is double the number from 1960. For the first time in our nation's history, the majority of adults are unmarried. One could certainly argue that being alone is not the same thing as being lonely, and yet so many people report that they have fewer and fewer people they can confide in. It seems ironic that as more and more digital networks allow us to be connected 24/7, fewer and fewer people seem to feel truly known and loved.

There are many ways to counter this trend, but it requires a profound sense of humility to see that we are not ours alone, and that living in relationship requires sacrifice, even as it brings joy.

For example, I may wish I had more "me time." I work hard all week, have a fairly long commute, and when I'm home at night and on the weekends it might be nice to hibernate in my bedroom, spend hours at a time online or reading, and eat on my own time. After a while, though, my family and friends would feel neglected and distant. My neighbors would notice I hadn't tended my yard. Things I love about my city, like its vibrant arts scene and community spirit, wouldn't be fostered or supported by me. Our democracy, which relies on participation, would have to look for others to keep it afloat. And forget the hungry, needy, and those in pain. They would have to find others to help them. Celebrations would have to go on without me. And I would eventually find myself walled off emotionally from everyone around me—an observer rather than a participant in life.

Being a part of a larger whole requires some effort, but it does not demand that we each become the same. I can preserve what is unique about me even as I enter into the space of committed relationships. In fact, it is our very differences that allow us to create community. One is brave, another nurturing; this one is handy while that one is creative. Wesley Ariaraje, a leading expert in interfaith dialogue, says that the first rule of living in a pluralist society is to respect the otherness of the other. If we can make space for our differences, we can live in peace together. We can be unique and known; self-expressed and yet accountable to others.

In 1942, American Baptist missionaries Clarence and Maude Josey Jordan took the extraordinary step of creating an interracial Christian community in the Deep South. Dubbed "Koinonia" to hearken back to the earliest Christian fellowships, they tried to emulate Jesus by sharing all their possessions, declaring the equality of all people, and embracing an ethic of good stewardship of the land. During the civil rights movement, their community withstood repeated bombings and a brutal economic boycott to survive even until this day. During his later years, Clarence Jordan created the Cotton Patch Parables, homey translations of the Christian scriptures. His translation of the "Good Samaritan," for example, updates the story of a nameless robbery victim, a Jew, who is rescued by an unlikely hero, a Samaritan, some two thousand years ago on the road to Jericho. In Jordan's version, an African-American man rescues a white victim of a beating on the road to Ellaville, Georgia, in the racially tense 1960s and takes the man to a white hospital at great personal risk. The story answers the question, "Who is my neighbor?"

> In order to answer this question, Jesus began to tell a story. While he was on his way from Atlanta down to Albany, some gangsters attacked a man. The robbers took the man's wallet, brand new suit, and drove away in his car. They left the poor man beaten and unconscious on the side of the road. Not long after this incident a "white preacher" came down the same road. When he saw the fellow, he stepped on the gas and went scooting by. Soon after this a "white Gospel song leader" came by and he too stepped on the gas. Then it so happened that a black man was traveling down this road and when he saw the fellow on the side of the road, he was moved to compassion and tears. Unlike the other two, he stopped and attended to his wounds and drove the man to the hospital in Albany. Then Jesus the Rebel asked the Bible teacher, "Which of these three would you consider to be your neighbor?" After the Bible teacher said, "The one who treated me kindly," Jesus said, "You get going and live like that!"

Circling back to 2013, I saw countless examples of Good Samaritans in the wake of the Boston Marathon bombing. Strangers jumped into the fray to help bind the wounds of others, not knowing if a third bomb would soon explode. Runners who could barely stand spent hours helping children find lost parents, and people throughout the city opened their homes for people who needed a place to stay. For a short time we were One Boston Strong—it was palpable in the subway stations and on the streets and in the places of commerce, as people made eye contact and shared stories and offered comfort to one another. Then, just a month later, we went mostly back to our protective New England city selves, but just mention that shared adversity and people break open once again.

A different world is possible. A more peaceful, just, and joyful world is possible. We can remember our more authentic, connected selves, but this requires something more than momentary heroics or even the shared aftermath of grief and loss. It requires the discipline of a regular spiritual practice to support the remembering of our deep belonging to one another and our world and to that transcendent power of Love. For some this practice can be found in joining a religious community and allowing the experience of shared worship to orient the heart outward. For others, it may mean embracing a private daily practice like meditation or prayer, and then translating that practice into some form of community engagement, such as the arts or social justice movements.

I am more than a self alone. I, like you, belong to humanity, to the earth, to the Spirit of Life and Love. When we remember this transcendent aspect of being, we become capable of treating one another with the deepest respect and kindness. In the spirit of Clarence Jordan, and of Jesus the Rebel, "You get going and live like that!"

God with Skin On

DON SOUTHWORTH

In the early 1980s when I became serious about learning about spirituality and doing my best to become a whole and loving human being, one of my gurus was Leo Buscaglia. He was a professor at the University of Southern California and a regular on PBS whose passionate, humorous message was all about love. He was funny and engaging and told stories about life and love that inspired millions of people to live more fully. Including me.

He was not a man of few words, which is why I've always been struck by a particular essay of his. He wrote how he dreamed of one day standing up to deliver a lecture to a group people who paid good money to hear him speak and saying simply, "Love. Love. Love." And then he would sit down, having said everything he had to say.

As a preacher who has made his living standing up talking, I too have dreamed of standing up one Sunday morning and saying three words, such as "love, love, love," and then sitting down. If I had the courage and the humility I would write an essay that would simply say "blessings, blessings, blessings" and be done. But Leo Buscaglia I am not, and perhaps blessings are not as easily understood and practiced as love.

I should probably say right up front that I am a big fan of blessings. Giving them, receiving them—in all their wondrous and glorious ways and in all their mysterious and confusing ways as well. For as long as I can remember, before I heard the call to ministry in the mid-1990s, I have ended each email I write with the word *blessings*. Now that I'm a minister that probably is not too surprising to people who receive my emails, but when I worked in the corporate world it was a bit more unique. Some people would think my salutation was intended as an expression of my religion (not true), others thought I was a little weird (probably true), and others thought I was simply wishing them well (absolutely true).

The word *blessing* comes from the Latin word *benedicere,* which means "to speak well." The author and theologian Henri Nouwen writes, in *Life of the Beloved,*

> To give someone a blessing is the most significant affirmation we can offer. It is more than a word of praise or appreciation; it is more than pointing out someone's talents or good deeds; it is more than putting someone in the light. To give a blessing is to affirm, to say "yes" to a person's Belovedness.

Saying "yes" to a person's Belovedness may be my favorite type of blessing. This is the blessing of thanks we offer those who have given us the gift of their presence, the universal blessing of appreciation for someone's birth, the speaking out loud of the joy, the love we have for another. These types of blessings may be the most important we offer, and for some they are the easiest to give. For others it takes practice, even spiritual practice perhaps, to not only remember to look for another's belovedness and beauty but to acknowledge them as well. Blessings, of course, need not be spoken. They may be kept silent in the sanctuaries of our hearts and minds as well. But they sound so good to the ear and our souls, why keep them to ourselves?

Giving blessings away, whether out loud or silently, is an important part of living a joyful life, and yet it is only one side of the spiritual coin. We humans are both blessers and blessings. Sometimes we forget that. What does it mean to be a blessing, and how do we remember and invoke the spirit of God and life that blessed us into being?

I remember the first religious community I joined when I was in my mid-twenties, the Home of Truth in Alameda, California. I rarely attended church when I grew up (Christmas and Easter only), but after beginning a spiritual awakening when entering recovery at age twenty-one and getting married with a growing family, I was hungry to find a place where blessers and blessings abounded. The small trans-denominational church was a place where I learned the joys and challenges of religious community and was taught, and occasionally reminded, that God and blessings take many forms.

As an extrovert who loves people, giving blessings has come more easily to me than the deeper acknowledgement and work of remembering that I am a blessing, delivered to this world and held in the arms of something much larger than I can fathom. On some days I call this God, on others I call it grace, and sometimes I simply laugh or cry in bewilderment. When I think about the experience of being blessed by this greater force I remember a song we sang every Sunday to close the service. The minister encouraged us to hold hands and sing, "I behold the Christ in you, I thank you for being in my life, I behold the Christ in you."

The song had more words but those are the ones I most remember. Although *Christ* was a word that I had issues with at the time, the simple act of holding someone's hands, looking into their eyes, and being reminded of the Christ, the God, the love in me (and them) moved me to tears almost every time. The practice, the reminder, transcended the issues I had with the word *Christ*. Because that deep knowing of our divinity always transcends words.

Many say that until we love ourselves we cannot truly love another. I'm not sure if that's true, but I do know that the more we love ourselves the deeper and healthier our love for others can be. I suspect the same can be said about blessings. The more we are able to cultivate an awareness and gratitude for the blessing we are in the world—and comprehend that we are manifestations of

something that transcends our limited scope of understanding—
the better we can reflect that to the world.

"May all beings without exception be happy." I first heard this
Buddhist blessing invoked at an interfaith gathering many years
ago. It has stuck with me as a simple blessing I can offer the world
and my fellow travelers anytime, anywhere, any day.

The Sanskrit word *namaste* is used as a greeting and salutation
in India. There are subtle differences in the definition of the word,
but the best I can decipher from the original Sanskrit is, "I bow to
the divine in you." Although I rarely say *namaste* to another out
loud, I invoke it frequently in my heart. Bowing to the divine in
you, in the mirror, in the backyard, in the cubicle at work, or in the
pew at church will deepen your relationships, even with yourself.

Perhaps you say a family grace before each meal. Or you wake
up in the morning and bow to the rising sun and give thanks for a
new day. Maybe you sit with your favorite morning beverage and
read a poem or prayer. Or you write in a gratitude journal before
going to sleep at night. Our days can be full of activities we check
off our to-do lists, or they can be sacred opportunities to remember the blessing we are and the blessing we wish to be to the world.

The mystic Meister Eckhart writes, "If the only prayer we say is
thank you that would suffice." Blessings are ways to say thank you
to God, the world, and those around us for the joys and sorrows,
ups and downs, of life. The truth is that we have nothing to do
with having been given this great gift of life. And while we can be
grateful for it, celebrate it, love it with all our hearts, we know that
we had nothing to do with it. Life is a blessing, something that has
been given to us without any strings clearly attached—except, perhaps, to give away our blessings without strings attached as well.

Blessings are the ultimate reminder that we are not alone. We
depend on others for the life we have been given and for the life we
wish to create and pass on. For those who celebrate the doctrine
of "I came into this world alone and will leave it alone," blessings
mess up the formula. If life, and/or perhaps God, is a blessing with
a capital "B," the random acts of kindness, thanksgiving, affirma-

tion, and love we pass on—the small "b" blessings—might be our way of saying "thank you" for the big B. In this way we become mediators and messengers of the spirit.

We are blessers, we are blessings, and we are blessed. The quality and richness of our lives is deepened when we not only remember this but, more importantly, when we practice it. How—and who—do you bless? Where do you turn for your blessings, and how are you a blessing in the world? What are the blessings in your life, and where are the blessings in disguise that are hard to see? These questions are worthy of our reflection, our study, our discussion, our life.

One of the greatest joys of being a minister has been the part of my job when I offer blessings: formal blessings in worship services, at rites of passage such as child dedications, weddings, and memorial services; informal blessings such as sitting in silence at a hospital bed, saying grace over a meal, sharing a laugh in a meeting, or encouraging and reminding someone of their greatness. These are the moments, the blessings, when I remember how powerful it can be to simply be present with and for another.

Some people think that because I have "Reverend" in front of my name my blessings, my words, my presence are touched with more of the divine. But they aren't. I have chosen, or been chosen, to do work that challenges me to bless people and situations often. And while I have been trained to invoke, practice, and, hopefully, remember blessings more regularly than someone who works in the corporate world, as I once did, I know now, more than ever, that all blessings and blessers are touched with the divine.

I try never to forget this. I greet each day with a prayer of gratitude asking that I might be, in St. Francis's words, "an instrument of thy will." I surround myself with pictures and words from people who inspire me and remind me of the joy, beauty, and sorrow of life. Instruments of grace and God, blessings that remind me that while divinity is born and resides in us, it is best displayed when we share it with others. The images include family, friends, Martin Luther King Jr., Gandhi, Willie Mays, St. Francis, Michelangelo,

Santa Claus. Sunrises. Sunsets. Hubble telescope photographs. Some people may look at these people and pictures and see only people and pictures. I see God. I see blessings—which may be one of the secrets to living a blessed life.

There was a time when I didn't write "blessings" on all my emails. When I didn't wake up and say a prayer or strive to live like those who have made a difference in the world. When I looked at a sunset and yawned or at a picture from space and felt even smaller and more insignificant than I already did. Or would be faced by the pains, troubles, and sorrows of life and want to throw in the towel instead of looking for the grain of hope and learning I might find.

I experienced a gradual awakening to the beauty and wonder around and inside me. Being in a community of people struggling to find and give blessings helped me to learn what was possible and how I might, one day, see blessings where I saw none and pass them on to others. Life is hard. It is full of sorrow and injustice that can be so overwhelming that we can lose hope. Which is why it is so crucial that we dedicate our lives to looking for blessings and passing them on. A friend of mine used to say that she needed to be around some people, or, "God with skin on them." Blessings are my kind of god with skin on them.

Rebecca Parker, recently retired president of Starr King School for the Ministry, wrote the poem "Choose to Bless the World," which I keep on my altar at home. It reads, in part,

> The choice to bless the world is more than an act of will
>   a moving forward into the world
> with the intention to do good.
> It is an act of recognition,
>   a confession of surprise,
>   a grateful acknowledgement
> that in the midst of a broken world
> unspeakable beauty, grace and mystery abide.

And so it is. Or, in other words, "blessings, blessings, blessings."

EXERCISES

Whose Are You?

You will need:
- movable chairs
- chime or smartphone with a gong application
- timekeeping device

Sit in pairs, each person facing a partner.
1. One asks, "Whose are you?"
2. Partner responds with a short phrase or word that comes to mind.
3. Questioner says, "God be merciful. Whose are you?"
4. Partner responds again with a short phrase or word that comes to mind.

The questioner does not react or respond to what is said, but simply receives. The responder does not fill the time with extra comments, even if there is silence between the question and any answer that may emerge. If both people fall into silence, they should simply wait attentively until the bell is rung.

Continue in this way until the bell rings. (Timekeeper: Ring bell after 5 minutes.) When the bell rings, the pair reverses roles. (Timekeeper: Ring bell after an additional 5 minutes.) When finished, each person asks the other: Were there any surprises in your responses?

Note: If you are working with this alone, you can write the exercise in a journal. On one side of the page write "Whose are you?" and on the other side write your short phrase or word that answers the question, then repeat. You can conclude with a prayer of thanks for all to which you belong.

Journaling

Write your answers to the question "Whose are you?" as often as you can throughout the month. Before coming to the next group meeting, look at your answers to see if there are any surprises or insights.

TWO

Who/What Calls Me?

You have a journey to make, a sacred journey, that I hope you'll eventually come to understand as a path to follow. This will be the most important thing you've ever done. Call it the "call of God," call it the "call of the Spirit," call it the "call of the Great Mystery," call it a "catastrophe," call it whatever you like, but a "call" of some kind is hidden within the troubles. The purpose of this call may be to draw out something hidden and wonderful within you, and if you don't mind me saying so, to bring about your awakening from a kind of spiritual slumber. I should tell you now: the journey ahead may not follow a very straightforward path, with clear-cut steps to take and easily identifiable problems to solve. Why? Because the foundation of your life, the core of who you believe yourself to be, is shaking quite a bit. It doesn't really matter how secure or insecure you believe that foundation is. It is unnerving and outright scary when this happens. At the same time, all those doubts about yourself and questions about God are evidence of a Great Mystery at work within you.

—Jeff Golliher, *A Deeper Faith*

Introduction

The life of the spirit is a life of purpose. When we name the ongoing purpose in our lives that moves us forward and remains a constant even when everything else changes, we come to know that we are on a sacred journey. Articulating and expressing that purpose, and identifying its continued movement in our lives, is crucial to making good decisions. We start with the experience of purpose as individuals and begin to see what we have in common with those who walk with us as pilgrims of the spirit.

Pour the Living Waters In

JON LUOPA

Several years ago I took part in a pastoral leadership program at Seattle University's School of Theology and Ministry. The participants included an ecumenical mix of clergy and were well balanced regarding gender, race, sexual orientation, and ethnic background. Each clergyperson had been in ministry for at least ten years. The program focused on what sustained each of us in our life and work.

Over the ten months of the program we worked with a variety of consultants and seminary professors. Once a month we attended a luncheon at which a local veteran clergyperson reflected on his or her vocation. These noontime gatherings were among the highpoints of the program for me.

At one of the luncheons our guest was Father Michael Ryan, the priest at the Catholic cathedral. He was a man widely respected in the community for his broad and inclusive spirit. He had been ordained during the heady days of the Second Vatican Council and, like so many of his fellow priests at the time, looked forward to seeing great change in his church. But now, more than forty years later, he reported that many in his church, especially younger priests, were eager to erase the gains of that early period and return the church to its traditional moorings.

One of the members in our program, assuming that the priest was discouraged as he was nearing retirement, asked him, "As you look back over your life's work, what sustains you now?" This seemed an appropriate question, coming from a group of clergy trying to rediscover what sustained them in their ministries.

Father Ryan gave an astonishing answer. Presuming that the person who asked him the question may have misunderstood him, the priest redirected the conversation. He said, "My prayer life. Because in it I cannot forget whose I am." He did not want us to think that all you need is a spiritual practice nor did he want this conversation to be about his personal effectiveness, sense of frustration, or legacy. The resolution of his own personal struggle would not be what sustained him. The priest chose to frame his answer in a larger context and this brought the conversation to a much deeper level.

Father Ryan answered as a priest should answer. In effect, he said, "I have given my life to the priesthood and the priesthood is my context. There is no such thing as 'my' priesthood. There is only the priesthood. And that body serves God and God's church. Whether or not I get discouraged is of no lasting consequence. If I get discouraged, I pray and by so doing remember that this calling is bigger than myself. As a priest my ego is subsumed by the bodies (the priesthood and God) to which I freely assent. That relationship confers dignity and worth to me."

This may be a foreign concept to those of us in a liberal religious tradition that holds the individual as sacrosanct. Our religious practice encourages individual expression. We take pride in the ways in which we differ from one another. Nevertheless, I was deeply moved by Father Ryan's answer at that luncheon. It invited us to ponder the implications. I wondered, "Whose am I as a Unitarian Universalist minister?" Whose are we as Unitarian Universalist ministers? To whom or to what am I bound in a way that both subsumes and dignifies my identity at the same time? As I entertained answers to these questions in my mind, I wondered if we Unitarian Universalists possess enough common vocabulary to talk about such things. Or are we confined by our individual idioms of definition? Do we share a common center that claims us, or are we nothing more than a community of proliferating differences?

I have wrestled with these questions for many decades. I have known to whom I belong since my ordination more than thirty years ago. But my answers to these questions seem not to be widely shared, and at times they have been openly ridiculed by colleagues and congregants. I understood what Father Ryan said. I know that I belong, in varying senses, to my family, to my congregation, to my colleagues, and to a liberal religious tradition. But these are all horizontal expressions of a vertical dimension. There is a transcendent dimension. I belong primarily to a God who is the Commanding Reality of life, commanding because it requires me to live in right relationship. This God is the transformative, sustaining, and redemptive power in the universe made known in relational experience. This God is both Source and Destiny, preceding and continuing beyond my brief existence. It is worthy of devotion and praise. It has staked a claim on my heart and my mind. And my hardest spiritual work is to accept that it has a loving intention for me and for all living creatures. Am I confined to the lonely task of answering the question, "Whose am I?" Or can we venture boldly and together answer the question, "Whose are we in the context of our liberal religious tradition?"

I told this story about the priest some years later during opening remarks at an Excellence in Ministry summit sponsored by the Unitarian Universalist Association and the Unitarian Universalist Ministers Association. In so doing I had hoped that we might spend some time at that gathering exploring whatever theological center we might have. The story was compelling enough that several ministers wanted to start a conversation right away. After the summit, some of these same ministers picked it up and developed a curriculum around it for further discussion among clergy in their local chapters, and later for use in congregational study groups.

Two ministers in each district were trained and sent back to their chapters to facilitate conversations among their colleagues. In my district we used two retreats to discuss these issues. After the retreats, colleagues shared that these had been among the most meaningful conversations they had had with their brothers and sisters in ministry, and that it was rare for ministers to discuss such personal, spiritual foundations.

In preparation for these retreats, I devoted two sermons to these topics. The response to the sermons surprised and gratified me. As I continued to talk about this in my congregation, folks who had been Unitarian Universalists for years felt that we were finally courageous enough to explore some of the questions and topics that had brought them to our fold in the first place. Young adults, most of whom had had no previous religious grounding, were delighted to be able to wrestle with these questions in a safe and nonjudgmental community. Our covenant groups used several of these themes for discussion over the course of a year. In our exploration classes for prospective members, we also hear very similar kinds of questions. People are looking for direction as they ponder to whom or to what they are accountable; by whom or what they want to be claimed. Is there anything that does or should claim us? People want to belong to something bigger than their personal selves. This may seem surprising, but many people are tired of searching. They don't mind searching if they also find something. Can we only encourage them to search alone, or can we try to find something like the common ground we all share?

There are signs all around us that we are not alone. Others, too, have had intimations of whose we are. I think of the words of Seth Curtis Beach in the hymn "Mysterious Presence, Source of All."

Mysterious Presence, source of all
The world without, the soul within
Thou fount of life, O hear our call
And pour thy living waters in.

Thou breathest in the rushing wind
Thy spirit stirs in leaf and flower;
Nor wilt thou from the willing mind
Withhold thy light and love and power.

That touch divine again impart
Still give the prophet's burning word
And vocal in each waiting heart
Let living psalms of praise be heard.

The surprising response of my colleagues at the ministry summit, as well as the responses from members of my congregation and colleagues in my local ministerial chapter, testify that we hunger to go theologically and religiously deeper. One person cannot profitably do that alone. We can best do this work in relationship with each other and with those sources that sustain us as individuals and as a people. I hear almost weekly from members and visitors that this is the principal reason they seek out and stay within our open and committed religious community.

As for me, I have a very different answer to the question I asked myself a few years back, "Whose are we as a Unitarian Universalist community?" At first I thought we were so idiosyncratic that little meaningful conversation was possible. How delightful it is to learn that my perspective is always partial and can be expanded by risking honest encounter with others. This is how I have come to experience the power of covenant in our midst.

Far from Ease and Grace

WILLIAM G. SINKFORD

The participants in the workshop lined up in the large room, shoulder to shoulder, in a physical metaphor of solidarity. The facilitator read a long list of statements that instructed each person to take steps forward or back if that statement described his or her life experience or identity.

> "If you do/have shopped with food stamps, take one step backward."
> "Won a scholarship to college, one step forward."
> "Have a visible or invisible disability, one step back."
> "A person of color, two steps back."
> "A light-skinned person of color, one step forward."
> "Loved by your parents, two steps forward."
> "If you are or appear male, two steps forward."
> "If you are transsexual, two steps back."

All of the usual categories were covered in some way: race, gender, sexual orientation and identity, ability, economic circumstance. The list of questions continued for a long time.

> "Told by strangers that you are handsome/beautiful, one step forward."
> "Raised by a single parent, one step back."

"Have or have had an addiction, one step back."
"Considered medically overweight/obese, two steps back."
"Victim of violence or abuse, two steps back."
"Family owned a second home, one step forward."

In response to the forty-five questions, the group had forty-five chances to move either forward or back. Everyone stepped both forward and backward more than once. Still, the group separated with a few persons far "ahead" and a few far "behind." At the end of the exercise, most clustered more or less near the original line. As the group reflected on the result, the facilitator and the group paid particular attention to those at the very back and far in front.

I've done this exercise several times. Known as "the dance of privilege," it has become common in "diversity" trainings in recent years. These particular questions are drawn from a curriculum called the "Beloved Conversations," created by Mark Hicks of Meadville Lombard Theological School.

Each time I've taken part, I've ended up on the positive side of the line. Not nearly as far ahead as some, but still ahead.

The privileges and positive regard I have experienced as a tall, well-educated, straight male tend to outweigh the painful experiences that have come with being a person of color, raised by a single mom, from modest economic circumstances. It is a reminder for me of how blessed I have been in my life. Not to be grateful would deny who I am.

I have experienced prejudice and projection, when the identities that are a part of who I am have led people to diminish me or—often even more painfully—to assume they understand all of who I am.

At times in my life, I have experienced those "two steps back" circumstances as deficits, somehow problems to be overcome. On better days, I know that this impulse simply reflects my own buy-in to the values we place on these categories. We are all complicit, to some extent, in maintaining the power of these categories.

I do not believe that oppression and suffering are redemptive in any meaningful sense. And yet I would not be the person I am without the challenges I have experienced, nor would I be able to empathize as easily with others who live out of different life experiences. It is in our responses to the challenges we face—not the challenges themselves—where we find hope.

In liberal religious circles, and progressive circles generally, it can sometimes feel that more privileged persons almost "need" my suffering. I don't claim to understand this. Perhaps empathy requires some measure of guilt. Perhaps those most privileged long for some forgiveness made possible by hearing the stories of those who have lived more challenged lives. Perhaps hearing of my struggles offers hope that their challenges can be faced as well, that their yearning for wholeness might be fulfilled.

What I do know is that no one of my identities, nor all of them added together, defines who I am. No one of your identities defines you. Real life is richer and far more complex than that.

Being a person of color has allowed me to benefit from any number of "affirmative action" moments. While it is true that I have been pulled over for DWB (driving while black), my experience is vastly different from that of someone without my education, income, "normative" English, and professional credentials.

Being a man has benefitted me in ways I know and in ways I'm sure I still cannot see. But there are experiences I will never have as a result of my gender and so I have a different—not better or worse, but different—relationship to the cycles and seasons of life.

I've encountered some new categories in recent years. I'm not sure how this happened, but there seems to be consensus that I am an elder. I certainly did not have that as a goal, but it has come to me and I am still trying to understand what that calls me to do. Do I get to take a step ahead or a step back as a result? With age have come some physical limitations that have heightened my awareness of "ability" as a category and experience.

I must confess that keeping track of all these identities, all these people in my person, tests me. I often get surprised when I am interacting with someone as their minister and find that they are looking at me as a person of color. I am both, of course. But when I allow myself to operate out of only one identity, I tend to miss things and get caught off guard.

There is a privilege in not having to pay as much attention to these identities that should be on that list of statements: "Don't have to think much about my identity, three steps forward."

Several years ago, a new minister of color was offered an internship at one of our largest congregations. The congregation had an explicit commitment to racial justice and hoped that this intern would offer a clarion call to justice-making from the pulpit. A "black" preaching style. Reach out to poor, person-of-color communities, attract persons of color to the pews, and build relationships with conservative clergy of color—all were on their wish list.

The intern was a devout humanist (if that is not an oxymoron), introverted, bookish, and from a well-to-do family who had lived almost her entire life in a "white world."

The internship was a disaster. The intern minister left Unitarian Universalism, and it took the congregation years to reclaim a mission that mentioned diversity. The racial justice advocates in the congregation were marginalized, and the called minister had repair work to do as well as managing his own feelings of inadequacy. The congregation's sense of failure became a significant spiritual issue.

I can critique the intern minister for saying "yes" to a call so out of keeping with her gifts. I can criticize the congregation's attempt to delegate their mission to an intern minister. But the more important lesson and challenge, as we navigate the tender territory where our calling meets the reality of our lives, is to resist seeing only what we want (or need) to see. That intern minister was well suited to serve the congregation as it was, but not to be the agent for the change they sought. Hope, like faith, can be blind.

I have more cautionary tales than success stories. Probably most of us do. The best we seem able to manage is to insist on attention to issues of privilege and oppression. Even those words feel weighty. We have come far enough to recognize that a diversity of experiences in our religious community enriches our lives.

We prioritize having voices from various categories represented on leadership groups and planning teams. There is value in all that. But we are far from ease and grace. Our efforts seem awkward and somewhat artificial. We operate with an abundance of caution, lest we offend or unintentionally exclude. As a result, our efforts often feel labored, rather than liberating.

The congregation I now serve, First Unitarian in Portland, Oregon, has a long history of welcome to and advocacy for gay and lesbian persons. Bisexual folks are present, though mostly silent. Transgender individuals are also present, and we are explicitly engaged in education about the varied life experiences imperfectly described by that broad category. We are beginning to ask, as a congregation, what we are called to do if our identity as a welcoming congregation is to have meaning. What do we do about those male and female restrooms?

But gay and lesbian folks and families have been welcomed for decades now. In fact, the growth of the congregation centers on the first days of my predecessor's ministry, now twenty years ago, when the church declared itself a hate-free zone and wrapped the block in red ribbon to demonstrate the point. The anti-gay ballot initiative that prompted those actions failed and the church exploded in attendance and membership. The very success of First Church as we know it today has that story at its center.

When I was called to ministry at First Church, I expected to find the Pride Group leading the charge for marriage equality in the state, with the strong support of large numbers of gay and lesbian members. I expected to find a hotbed of advocacy.

I found a community that was indeed a religious home for many gay and lesbian individuals and families. Many served in leadership positions—on the Board, in religious education, the annual canvas. That was routine and not worthy of mention.

But the Pride Group was small and as I began to get to know some of the gay and lesbian folks in leadership, what I heard surprised me. They talked about how important the church was in their lives, but not as a focal point for advocacy. What they prized most was having a religious home where they did not need to advocate, where they could be comfortable as who they were, without having to protest or march, without having to be the token gay on the committee or speak for the queer community.

Let me be clear that there is energy in our Pride Group. Soon Oregon will have the chance once more to approve marriage equality. I am certain that First Church will be a leading part of that education and advocacy effort. But the meaning of the congregation for many gay and lesbian members has much less to do with advocacy and more to do with ease, comfort, and grace.

Are we called to dream into reality a world where the particularities of experience are no longer weighted and freighted with such positive and negative value? Is that the step forward we long to collectively take? Should we try to build a land in which human experience is so homogenous that the categories lose their power and meaning?

Since President Obama's election we have all read the speculation—or is it a hope?—that we are moving into a "post-racial" America. Similarly, the rapid change of attitudes toward the queer community and victories on anti-discrimination laws and marriage predictably raise our spirits. And moving toward more accessible facilities makes us proud.

There are powerful generational differences. Younger middle-class Americans have grown up assuming diversity of race and culture as the norm. And for most of them, marriage equality is a no-brainer. How will they deal with these traditional categories of identity when their experiences are so different? Will they find ways to teach and challenge those in my generation about the impact of income and class? The impact of living in a developed versus a developing society?

To be sure, the traditional categories are still with us. Our world is not "post-racial" when the killer of a young black man walking home from the store with a bag of candy walks free. Marriage equality is a reality in only a dozen states. Bullying is rampant in our schools. There are too many examples to list; there is much justice yet to be achieved.

From deep in our religious DNA we hear the call to prevent violence to the body and spirit. A faith of deeds not creeds must answer that call, or we are false prophets and hypocrites.

We are called by and toward a vision of the beloved community, but we are also called out of and from our own experiences. We can ask, How we can use our own experiences of being pressed down, and we all have them, to cultivate a capacity for empathy and tolerance for the messy and sometimes painful practice of solidarity. How can we use our own experiences as tools and not simply relegate them to the category of "troubles we have overcome"?

The religious task exists not only in the realms of advocacy and public policy. As much as we are called to help heal the wounded world, we are also called to find some meaning and peace in our own lives. "Our spirits long to be made whole," in the words of a favorite hymn.

The Beloved Community

We know that to move toward that vision will require changes in public policy and our practice of community. It is a small and relatively easy step to advocacy when we allow ourselves to know how the structures in which we live (and the habits of our hearts) press down on the lives of others.

What calls us to embrace that vision? What voice shouts its imperatives or whispers the possibility that love might be real?

The God I know, and I use that word, does not "will" or insist that we live toward the vision of the beloved community. The God I know exists as a possibility or a potential that is present in my life and in which my life plays a part.

It is not the idea of wholeness but glimpses of wholeness that support me and give me hope. The times when I have felt the blessings in my life, and not just the obstacles I have faced. The times when I have, somehow, felt held when fear and grief might have overwhelmed me. My prayer life helps me remember those times. Re-member. Call them forth again.

We long for certainty, a blueprint we can confidently follow. What we get are glimpses.

Glimpses of Wholeness

Back in that room, where a community of souls did the "dance of privilege," the white man farthest in front turned and looked back. "I see now," he said and wept. The woman of color, living on food stamps, one of the farthest toward the rear, smiled when she was offered sympathy. "My life is not easy," she said "but living my life has given me strength."

We often call this process of finding and accepting our place in the world "work." "Diversity work," "the work of justice"—we all know those phrases and many of us use them. It requires intention and attention to know, as honestly as we can, the truth of our lives. But there is a place beyond "the work" where love and grace abide. We know it with the sharp intake of breath when we tell the truth of our lives and others know and bless that truth. We know it with the tears that sometimes come when silence moves us toward acceptance.

This must have been at least part of what Jesus meant when he said that the kingdom of God is already here, available to each of us, waiting to be born into the world through our lives. But language can only point to these moments when we know, in some way, that we belong and that our longing for wholeness is not an idle dream.

Glimpses of wholeness are not exclusive to the church. They come in 12-step meetings for some, or in practicing Tai Chi, listening to music, or walking in the woods for others. All these can offer intimations of the mystery that feels the beating of our hearts echo and amplify the pulse of the world. But the church is where we promise to make ourselves most available to them, to seek out those glimpses and to allow them to call us into living as we wish to live. And where the lives of others lift us toward that vision.

Commitment to the church is a practice, a discipline in which we choose to remind ourselves and remember, re-member, the possibility and hope we have glimpsed. In the wilderness of responsibilities, of failures of energy and of nerve, in the face of the tyranny of the to-do list, we choose to follow paths where we have glimpsed wholeness before. And even if what we find is just the memory of wholeness, it somehow sustains us.

It is not easy to have only glimpses of what we can rely on. I suppose that is why they call what we do "faith"—a belief that grace will come as we answer the call to take one more step forward.

EXERCISES

Experiencing Your Call

You will need:
- movable chairs
- chime or smartphone with a gong application
- timekeeping device

Begin by pairing up with a partner. Reflect on the following questions, alternating roles of speaker and listener:

- Describe your experience of call. It may not have been a dramatic moment. Is there a time when you have realized how your gifts meet the world's need? Or how you have moved toward wholeness and been blessed?
- Where did your call come from? What was its source? If you describe it as a voice, was it from within or outside yourself? Or both? How has it been shaped by your ethnicity, gender identity, sexual orientation, class, race, or age? How has it been affected by the claims that come to us from the future, which are not yet realized?

Next, if your group numbers eight or more people, gather in groups of four. Otherwise, gather as a whole group. Sit in silence for thirty minutes until the facilitator rings the chime. Then, have participants speak reflectively and attentively about the shape of their call.

Finally, gather together as a whole group if you had been in groups of four. Share briefly as a large group, reflecting on these questions:

- Did you find any common threads as you talked with your partner and in your group of four/whole group?
- Were there any surprises?

Journaling

Write or draw something that might parallel the priest's comment in Jon Luopa's essay, "Pour the Living Waters In" (page 19). This could be something that is your purpose or call that is beyond your present daily life or circumstances. What possesses you? Who tells you who you are? To whom or what do you belong in the sense that Father Michael Ryan belonged, even when his church failed his hopes and the purposes of his priesthood seemed unfulfilled? Who or what sustains you when you are discouraged about your life or when you feel betrayed by your deepest commitments?

THREE

Living the Call

And Jacob was left alone; and a man wrestled with him until the breaking of the day. When the man saw that he did not prevail against Jacob, he touched the hollow of his thigh; and Jacob's thigh was put out of joint as he wrestled with him. Then he said, "Let me go, for the day is breaking." But Jacob said, "I will not let you go, unless you bless me." And he said to him, "What is your name?" And he said, "Jacob." Then he said, "Your name shall no more be called Jacob, but Israel, for you have striven with God and with men, and have prevailed." Then Jacob asked him, "Tell me, I pray, your name." But he said, "Why is it that you ask my name?" And there he blessed him. Jacob called the name of the place Peni'el, saying, "For I have seen God face to face, and yet my life is preserved." The sun rose upon him as he passed Peni'el, limping because of his thigh.

—Genesis 32:24–32

"The deeper we get into reality, the more numerous will be the questions we cannot answer."

—Friedrich von Hügel, *Letters to a Niece*

Introduction

Discerning what our call requires of us in the context of our daily lives can be challenging. As we acknowledge the tensions inherent in our sacred journey, we recognize that we don't have to resolve the tensions to be faithful to our purpose. Having a prayer life can help us respond to the paradoxes we experience while being faithful to our call.

The Boots Worked Either Way

BRET LORTIE

In 1984 I joined the U.S. Air Force right out of high school, and for the first time I began to understand some of the deep contradictions of our world. In a boot camp briefing we learned about the nuclear madness of the Cold War. The training instructor called it M.A.D., for "mutually assured destruction." If we knew it was madness, I wanted to ask, why didn't we do something to change it? I had long been aware of the nuclear dangers of our world. Near my home growing up, Rockedyne used to test rocket engines that would shake the windows of my school. I felt certain that the roar of those engines was what a nuclear blast would sound and feel like just before we got vaporized. I always felt better a few minutes after the roar ended, once I was sure it was a rocket test and not the apocalypse.

Later, I lived the madness. Six months into my active duty service, I started working the night shift, inspecting airborne command posts for Project Looking Glass, the EC-135 aircraft from which America's arsenal of nukes would be launched after Washington, Norad, and Strategic Air Command headquarters had been destroyed. I worked at Strategic Air Command HQ. Our wing flew twenty-four hours a day, seven days a week—so that even after I'd been turned to vapor, the United States could still launch a second strike.

As my awareness grew, so did my feeling that I was caught up in something wrong. On the one hand I remained proud of serving my country, especially the Air Force, and the sky-blue uniform I wore. On the other, I became so opposed to nuclear weapons that I switched political parties, starting reading "subversive" publications (which I sometimes pulled out at lunch to shock my sergeant), and in my off-duty hours enrolled in journalism school at the local university. By day, an undergrad in a punk rock t-shirt; by night, an airman wearing a battle dress uniform. The combat boots looked the part either way.

Paradoxically, I could authentically inhabit both identities simultaneously. When my active duty commitment ended, I even re-enlisted in the Air National Guard so I could continue serving while finishing my journalism degree. At that time I also became more involved in peace and activist work. The paradox continued.

After seven years of military service and several working in the printing industry, my aspirations as a journalist came full circle when I got hired by the *Bulletin of the Atomic Scientists* to write and edit articles on nuclear affairs and arms control. The magazine, part of the concerned scientists movement, was devoted to ridding the world of nuclear weapons. I was hired, my editor told me, not in spite of my military service and familiarity with the U.S. nuclear machine, but because of it. I had lived in both worlds.

I entered seminary back in 2002, and I'm fairly certain that the September 11 bombings in New York had something to do with that decision. If the world was truly going to pieces (now because of terrorists rather than Russian nukes), I thought the best I might do is hunker down in religious community. To preach and teach, and write! I wanted to explore what it meant to make the most of this life, for ourselves and humanity. Of course, becoming a minister just set up new polar tensions in which to live: between contemplation and action; between the prophetic word and servant leadership; between loving the world and loving it enough to want to change it. Amid these new tensions I often feel the most alive and engaged.

Yet the old tensions remain. In my closet at home, hanging next to my robes and stoles, is the same uniform that I wore while on active duty—now adorned with a chaplain's cross. Today I serve in the Air Force's volunteer auxiliary, the Civil Air Patrol, but when I wear my "blues" for summer training or encampment, a memorial service for a downed pilot, or a public event, I have that same deep sense of both pride and humility in representing the United States in my small way. I also remain aware of the complexities and historical failings of the military industrial complex. I get giddy at an F-16 flyover, yet incensed at the sight of a Predator drone.

This paradox becomes more acute for me each June at General Assembly (GA) when I'm required by the Unitarian Universalist Association's military endorser to wear my uniform to designated public events, such as the Service of the Living Tradition, in order to visibly support our Unitarian Universalist military chaplain corps. As another chaplain once put it, "the endorser needs boots on the ground," or at least uniforms on the floor. Each year I get a few subtle or not-so-subtle comments regarding the incompatibility of our faith with my uniform.

This past year, as an official chaplain for the 2013 General Assembly, I felt such a critique directly when, sitting in the chaplain's office, two attendees walked in and wanted to talk about the "military invasion of GA." I can relate this without breaking confidentiality because they wanted the concern to be made widely public. Everywhere they looked, they said, it seemed the work of the military was being praised, and the work of peace activists was going unrecognized. As they sat down, they noticed my Air Force–style uniform hanging in the corner because I had just come from the President's reception thanking our military chaplains for their service. "Perhaps you aren't the right person to speak to about this," they suggested.

"If you're comfortable, I think I'm the best person for you to speak with," I replied. "I truly want to hear your experience." I explained I was on the UUA's Committee for Military Ministry, and therefore I might be able to bring their concerns right to the people who should hear them. They agreed.

We spent the next half-hour talking together, and then we invited the "right relations" team in to expand the conversation.

I don't know if we resolved the tension, but we certainly got to know one another better. We met in the middle. I was able to see the world, momentarily, through their eyes, and I noticed some inconsistencies that I had not seen before. I felt incredibly grateful for being able to feel the tensions inherent in our commitments to diversity, peace, security, freedom, and justice. Whether standing on the anti-war protest line (which I told my new activist friends that I've done) or supporting our troops from within the military community, I have lived a double life.

Our world is rife with tensions like these that tug and pull, and it seems the more open-minded we are, the more we are subjected to the inconsistencies and human failings that make life both interesting and frustrating. When people tell me about their discomforts with a world (or a church, a family, a relationship, etc.) that does not turn out as they expected, I often say that this is the result of being a thoughtful person. Feeling that discomfort doesn't mean we should jump off, or out, of these situations. The more we observe and accept, the more we become aware of the conflicting ideals embedded in our religious tradition, our national character, our personal habits, and even those in our own hearts. When we learn to accept these conflicts (AKA, "things as they are"), we find it easier to stay engaged and in relationship.

Some of us also live within the tensions of race, gender, or sexual identity. As a male of European descent who is married to a woman, I've had an easier time than many blending into the dominant Western culture and a harder time than some learning to listen and be present to the experiences of others that challenge my position of privilege.

I've learned that I'm not alone. For example, my congregation has explored its attitudes and biases regarding gender by going through the "Living the Welcoming Congregation" process. We've encountered tensions along the way—not so much around straight and gay or lesbian identities but with those identities with which we, collectively, are less familiar. I've heard many bisexual, transgender, queer, and questioning members express dissatisfaction with how our religious culture has mishandled the identities that don't fall within the traditional categories. I've heard people with a variety of orientations express frustration about having to break out of these categories.

Returning to my experience as a 2013 GA chaplain, the issue I heard about most wasn't the military presence but the gender-neutral bathrooms. These became the forum in which many of us confronted our own categorical thinking. The gender-neutral bathrooms were established in response to a number of attendees who pointed out that such binary distinctions as "male" and "female" didn't describe their experience of gender. They shared their experience of being challenged because they looked too feminine for the men's room or too masculine for the women's room.

We did the right thing by making several of our bathrooms gender neutral, but this issue brought the most people to the doors of the GA chaplain's office. As I listened to attendees process their experience about their adventures into the uncharted territories of urinals and sanitary canisters, I realized that their primary discomforts focused around understanding the non-binary gender associations they were being asked to consider—often for the first time. They felt pushed into their zones of discomfort, and this fouled them up more than politics or gender theory. As far as Association controversies go, it was a cake walk for me as a chaplain: a little listening, a few nudges toward compassion regarding the shared experience of being human, some gentle reminders of our values, and most chaplain visits ended well. I was encouraged by how much people wanted, in their heart of hearts, to confront their polar thinking and existing biases, even when it came to bathrooms.

All human systems create polar tensions, which produce paradoxes from having to live within those tensions. As with so many things, the problem of the paradox of living between poles contains its own solution and its power. When we become aware of the tensions in our lives, that awareness becomes a powerful ally—for with it we can find where our hearts are, even if for just that moment.

We don't have to feel the same way all the time. This isn't a mushy relativism but an admission that we are complex creatures often faced with irreconcilable desires: for security or peace; for stability or adventure; for communion or independence. We get into real trouble when we cling to one pole or the other. The question then becomes how can we listen to another person's story in a way that opens our hearts to their paradox.

I've often used music as a metaphor to explain how I grapple with all this. We may think we love "harmonious music," but harmony is only interesting when there's tension, even discord, within it. I remember in a music theory class, way back when, one of our first assignments involved composing chorales in four-part harmony. It's not that hard to compose a simple eight-bar chorale that sounds "nice." You can even work out the technical imperfections, such as finding the parallel fifths or octaves, or the technical difficulties, such as discovering where the voices cross. But try composing a chorale like Bach's, and you realize his genius lay in his counter-melodies, in the second voice that speaks from within a composition as a counterpoint to the first. Some composers are known for their melodies, others for their harmonies. Bach's melodies are equaled only by his harmonizations—that is, the beauty of the primary idea enhanced by the power of the second competing idea.

In his book *In Quest of Spirit*, avant-garde composer Jonathan Harvey says that music—because it is both emotionally intense and possessed of a deep harmony—disproves Aristotle's Law of the Excluded Middle, which says that a thing cannot be two things at once. This law declares that a thing must either be this or that, with nothing in between. Think of how many times this kind of dualism has gotten our world into trouble. Right versus wrong. Us versus them. Evil doers versus, well, who? But music offers us an alternative, Harvey says, for if it is to be meaningful, music must be more than one thing at a time. Beautiful and abrasive. Harmonious and dissonant.

As poet John Keats once put it in a letter to his brothers, art such as music must exist in ambiguity, must be full of "contradictions . . . uncertainties, mysteries, doubts, without any irritable reaching after fact and reason." When Harvey composes music, he says he pulls "together these dark conflicts and contradictions in an intuitive drive toward the promised land of unity."

Put another way, to produce music that has the power to move the listener, a composer has to exist within the paradox of music itself: We want to be satisfied by the resolution of a piece of music, yet without agitation within the concord, our intellects are left hungry for something real and life affirming. We hunger for both tension and resolution. Life in the paradox.

If music gives us a theoretical metaphor to understand tension, it still doesn't help us practice living within it. My primary way of learning to live within life's ambiguities is through the practice of insight meditation, although those with other contemplative practices describe achieving similar relief (what Theravada Buddhists call "the quenching or cooling of Dukkha") through *zazen*, yoga, *Qigong*, centering prayer, labyrinth walking, *lectio divina*, deep listening, and other activities that force one to observe how reactive the mind and body can be to the disorienting stresses of life.

The term *dukkha*, the Pali word for stress, is a useful concept— although even that translation is not completely adequate. *Dukkha* can also be translated as suffering, anxiety, and unsatisfactoriness.

While the translation may be unclear, the Buddha was not unclear about the presence of *dukkha* in our lives: "Now what, friends, is the noble truth of stress? Birth is stressful, aging is stressful, death is stressful; sorrow, lamentation, pain, distress, and despair are stressful; association with the unbeloved is stressful; separation from the loved is stressful; not getting what is wanted is stressful." In short, just being alive is stress enough for a lifetime of practice. Contemplative practice is one way to calm our minds, or at least understand better what our minds are doing.

"I'll bet your mind just calms down right away when you meditate," someone once said to me, a person I was encouraging to try meditation. "You're that kind of person."

"Nothing could be further from the truth," I replied. "I probably have five or ten minutes in a sitting where I experience some tranquility and bliss." The rest of the time I'm watching and working.

"Working?"

"Sure. It's work to keep herding those monkeys."

"Monkeys?"

"The Buddha described the human mind as filled with drunken monkeys that jump, screech, and chatter."

"That doesn't sound peaceful or fun."

"Exactly. Practice is work. Beneficial work, yes. But still work."

It's true. I sit. I center the breath. I might have a minute or two of soothing, deep inhalations and exhalations, and then the "monkey mind" begins. By getting to know the monkeys (because we'll never tame them, really), we find acceptance, compassion, and equanimity more accessible to us.

The better we get at accepting the monkeys that are right there in our heads, the better we get at accepting the world as it is. It's called "practice" for a reason. It's not something we get right or wrong, but something we get better at the more we do it. Once we learn to notice and accept the tensions within our own minds, we become better at noticing and accepting the tensions in the world.

When we learn to hold tension in this way, when we learn to recognize within ourselves why we get agitated when someone does something that runs counter to our reason (or defies all reason), we become better partners with others in making the world a better place. I've often heard it said that one reason old-time Unitarians came to church was to hone each another's reasoning ability and rhetorical skills—to argue for the sake of becoming better thinkers, or for the sport of it. If I could banish one practice from our faith, it would be that. We come together not to worship reason, or for the sake of reason alone, but to use our faculties to see the world as it is and then engage with it in ways that benefit others. Arguing to reach better conclusions, or to become better debaters, or to hone the thinking skills are just attempts to resolve the paradox and lessen our discomfort with tension. When we gather to understand each other's reasoning and hearts, then we become better agents of change.

What a better world we will create when we focus on understanding others rather than controlling them. In our communities of faith, our incubators of the spirit, we have the unique opportunity not just to observe the paradox of belief and our shared human condition, but to live into that paradox. We get to notice it, learn to relish it, and then resolve again to go out into the world and be with the world, as dusty and imperfect as it is.

The Outpouring of the Heart

CHERYL M. WALKER

I grew up in a religious tradition in which prayers were to be said at least five times a day. In Islam, prayer is the first thing one does after waking and the last thing one does before retiring for the day. Praying five times a day reminds us that we are always in relationship to God. The prayers, the way of praying, and the times of prayer are all prescribed. Truthfully, I was not very good at prayer. Rarely did I ever pray all five required prayers in a day, and over time I grew less and less comfortable with the words of the prayers. Like many young adults I questioned the very existence of the God to whom I was supposed to pray and soon found that I no longer prayed at all. I lost something that I wasn't sure I wanted or even needed.

What I thought I lost were words and rituals and God. What I really lost was a deep and abiding relationship to the Holy. Without that relationship the world felt like a lonelier place. While I had good relationships with many people, these were no substitute for a relationship with that which is greater than the sum of our parts. I missed prayer, or rather, I missed being able to connect to that greater energy that I knew existed but could not name.

Like Jacob, I wanted to know "What is your name?" I knew what it was not, but I did not know what it was. I could call it *God* but that word still kept me vacillating between the baggage of old images and having no belief in it at all. I needed to find a new way of seeing the holy; new words and new rituals in order to reclaim a new relationship with it. I needed a way to reclaim prayer.

It took a good friend, who is an avowed atheist, to give prayer back to me when she said, "I don't pray, but there are times when I sit and pour out what is in my heart into the universe." If there is a better definition of prayer than that, I am not sure what it is. Prayer is the pouring out of that which is in our hearts. It does not matter if we believe in God with a big G, or the Holy with a big H. It does not matter to whom or what we address our prayers, the only thing that matters is that which is in our hearts that needs pouring out.

Too often we get so stuck on the address that we are unable to get to the message. Prayer need not have an addressee, because it is the addresser that matters, for in prayer we know that, ultimately, we are the ones being changed. Whether we believe in a God who is transcendent (beyond us) or immanent (within us) or both or neither, the only thing we can know for sure is that we are transformed in prayer.

Prayer is an active process of becoming vulnerable so that we may be changed. In prayer we shed the clothes of persona and stand naked before the holy, however we define it. In prayer we do not seek to be our ideal selves; just who we are in the moment with all our beauties and all our flaws on full display. There is a great exposure in being just who we are, but we can be vulnerable in prayer because we are unconcerned with what others may think of us. In prayer we become detached from the expectations of others and ourselves. Alone in the darkness and light of relationship with the sacred mystery of our existence, we can openly confess who we are and that which is in our hearts.

It takes practice or calamity to let go of our ideal selves and become vulnerable in prayer. It's probably preferable to engage in a practice than to wait for a calamity, though a calamity often brings us to vulnerability much quicker. In prayer we learn to let go of the ideal version of ourselves and fully face the reality of who we are. It takes time for us to be able to confess ourselves as beautifully flawed. In the beginning we may only see our beauties or only see our flaws, neither of which is the whole truth of our existence. We may be fearful of who we might actually find when we look, clearly, into the mirror, and so we are tempted to see only one side of ourselves. We may confess our sins and fail to see our graces or we may extol our strengths and ignore our weaknesses. Through the practice of prayer we learn to pray ourselves into the tension between our best and worst selves, which is where we live. We learn to wrestle within the space of who we are and who we are not.

As our practice of prayer evolves over time, it becomes easier to confess who we truly are, to be vulnerable to ourselves and whatever we may name as holy. When we learn to be vulnerable, we can move from confession to petition and state our needs. We can ask the question, "How can I be changed that I might live well in the space between the tensions in my life?" Our ultimate purpose in prayer is not to change the tensions but to change ourselves so we can live gracefully within their limits.

In our lives we face many tensions between the ideal and reality. We want to treat everyone with dignity and respect, and yet there are people who do evil deeds and we question their worth. We want to be kind and caring, yet sometimes we feel anything but kind and caring. We feel called to do good in the world, yet our deeds constitute more of the problem than the solution. We want to travel our own road, but our commitments and responsibilities limit the roads from which we can choose. The list goes on and on; each of us has tensions in our lives that we wish would just go away but they don't.

Prayer allows us the time and space to look at these tensions, to seek reconciliation with them, and to be changed in ways that may also allow us to resolve some of them. Just as we need to truthfully confess who we are in prayer, we also need to truthfully name our tensions. When we remember that our ultimate goal is not to avoid the tensions but to live well within their limits, we free ourselves to name them truthfully and see them honestly. In prayer there is no judgment placed upon our tensions; one is not good, nor the other bad. Placing a value on the tensions says more about our ideal vision of the world than its reality. When we strip away the values we place on our tensions, we can see them for what they really are. They may be choices we have made that we feel conflicted about. They may be choices we must make that we do not wish to make. They may be two sides of the same coin. They may represent our full range of human emotions. In our prayer practice we learn to remove the values we have placed on our tensions in order to see them clearly.

Once we truly know ourselves and our tensions, we may then seek the path of reconciliation. This process also requires practice —a practice of patience. Prayer is not a quick fix. We can't enter into prayer thinking we'll just sit and pray for a couple minutes or even hours and then, when we're done, all our problems will be solved and we'll know just what to do. Since prayer is a process that changes us, we must learn to have the patience to be changed, slowly and gradually. Even if we do pray five times a day, we cannot hasten that process. Through prayer, we are not instantly changed; we are opened to being changed. We become trusting enough to be vulnerable, detached enough to see clearly, and only then open enough to be changed.

During this process, we may feel a deep gratitude. We are not grateful for the change to come, which would be presumptuous, but for the fact that we can be transformed. As long as we have breath, we have the ability to be transformed, and for that we can be grateful—grateful that we may gracefully pray ourselves into our tensions and courageously pray ourselves into reconciliation. We emerge from prayer with a new way of living within our tensions. Some of them will never go away; we may always get pulled in different directions. Some of them we will see differently because we have changed our perspective, and we may then find ways to resolve them. Prayer doesn't fix things and it doesn't fix us. It opens up new ways for us to experience our lives, the world, and the holy; then we may consciously fix things.

The process of prayer is individual. Some people find it helpful to have a quiet space in their home for prayer, others may find prayer time during a walk in the woods, while still others may pray on the treadmill at the gym. Some may need stillness while others need their bodies to be in motion. Some find writing their prayers to be helpful while others use art. The prayer exercises that follow this essay are included not as a prescription for your prayer life but as one way to engage the process. You will ultimately decide what form your prayer practice will take. The form is not as important as is taking the time to do it. The one thing we need for prayer is time. Prayer connects us to whose we are, and connection takes time.

I still don't always pray five times as day; some days it is more, some days it is less, and some rare days not at all. And I still don't have specific times of the day that I pray, though I do try to make it the first and last things I do. And I don't have specific words that I pray each time. I have no prescriptions for the form my prayers will take. But I do have a practice and when tensions arise between my needs and desires, between my time and my call, between my ideal and my reality, I am able to pray myself into the tensions, knowing that eventually I will pray myself into reconciliation so that I may gracefully live with them.

EXERCISES

Recognizing the Tensions

You will need:
- journal or paper for each participant
- pens and/or pencils

The group leaders begin by explaining that we experience many tensions in our lives. Some of these include:

Freedom	and	Authority
Utopian ideals	and	Political reality
Righteousness	and	Tolerance
Independence	and	Communion
Personal	and	Covenantal
Journey	and	Home
Fear	and	Love

The leaders then provide some other examples from their own experience. (It is important to remember that the desire to resolve these tensions can sometimes distort our perception of how to live with them.)

Group participants take some time to reflect on one or two tensions they are experiencing themselves. Then the leaders invite the participants to name some of these tensions out loud.

After sharing together, each participant takes out some paper and a pen and writes or draws a prayer about one or more of the tensions in their lives. Then, as moved to do so, they read aloud or describe their prayers.

Leaders conclude with a prayer that recognizes the tensions in our lives and asks that we might have the grace to support one another as we live within them.

Journaling

Write a conversation between you and the Holy as you wrestle with the tensions in your life. Write both sides of that conversation.

FOUR

Our Covenants

Love is the doctrine of this church,
The quest of truth is its
sacrament,
And service is its prayer.

To dwell together in peace,
To seek knowledge in freedom,
To serve human need,
To the end that all souls shall
Grow into harmony with
the Divine—

Thus do we covenant with each
other and with God.
—arranged by L. Griswold Williams

The Pilgrims ought to be especially important to American Unitarian Universalists. They are our spiritual ancestors. We misapprehend our own identity and miss out on a great richness if we do not understand our derivation from their extraordinary spirit. I believe we could much diminish the fruitless and sterile individualism among us and instead foster together far richer varieties of authentic individuality in community if we could, through the seventeenth-century Pilgrims, set about reclaiming, for today, a fresh, dynamic commitment to the spirit of the covenant of the free church. . . .

The center of the free church, the heart of the whole thing,
is a promise of fidelity, a covenant, which each member
freely makes upon joining. Actually also, each member
begins again with, or renews or renegotiates, his or her
promise many times in the course of the life of the church,
in the privacy of renewed conscience or spiritual growth.
Too often our promise, or covenant, is implicit, not consciously explicit. But it doesn't really matter whether it is
verbalized. It matters whether it is faithfully meant.

—Alice Blair Wesley, *Redeeming Time*

Introduction

The church lies at the intersection of the Holy and the covenant
that calls us into relationship with one another. Covenants order
our lives by expressing the commitments we make to each other
and to God, that deepening power that beckons us to lead lives
of faithful purpose. We are defined by our promises that establish
how we are in right relationship. We grow in spiritual maturity
as we remain faithful to the primary relationships we establish
through our covenants as members of a congregation, and as we
recognize how these relationships are at work in our lives now.

Open the Door and There Are the People

LISA K. JENNINGS

Many of us have heard the old joke about the minister who said, "This job would be really great if it weren't for all the people." Well, that's the way it is in many aspects of our lives. Life would be great if it weren't for certain people we have to deal with, but we just can't get away from people. Life is made up of others all around us. And as we come to we define ourselves in our relationships with other people, the importance of covenant becomes paramount in our lives.

The beginnings of covenant as we know it in the modern world originated as a bond between God and his people, as chronicled in Genesis and Exodus. Being in covenant entails being in right relationship with the holy or God (the vertical dimension of covenant relationship) and with other people (the horizontal dimension). Thus, right relationship involves, first and foremost, attending to the ways of that which is holy and defining what is true in our lives. Paying attention to the Holy can enlarge our gratitude and generosity of spirit and help us prioritize that which is most important to us. In essence, the vertical dimension calls for our hopes and dreams for the world.

Developing these fundamental attitudes or values does not happen easily or quickly. We need to practice cultivating right intention and generosity of spirit. We are truly a work in progress. Faithfulness to that which we call holy and true involves expanding our hearts in both the vertical and horizontal dimensions. We can only grow in both dimensions by having an appreciative awareness of something beyond what we can describe and by being in right relationship with others.

Covenants that take the form of sincere agreements are made between persons or groups of people in the horizontal dimension, and they are typically affirming in nature. They encourage tranquility and bring stability to the world. They have three general characteristics. First, they are entered into willingly and without coercion. Second, they aspire to fidelity and commitment to truth and avoid the pursuit of behaviors that diminish its spirit. Third, they call for non-retaliation and a commitment to attempt to heal those broken by their efforts to cultivate a generosity of spirit. We must extend mercy to one another in covenant because all the members of the community of faith are making their way in the world only by grace. Developing a generosity of spirit is a faith practice that we must aspire to on a daily basis. As Jesus teaches in the Sermon on the Mount, one can differentiate the quality of the tree by the fruit it bears.

Covenant crosses all aspects of our lives but we mostly identify it within our inner circle of family and church community. Within the community of faith, we must make our way through external influences that continually challenge it—greed, skepticism, and oppression. As we ponder our life's work, we as Unitarian Universalists become increasingly aware that our legacy will be judged on the basis of our response to and care for not only those in our inner circle but also those most in need—the starving, the thirsty, the outsiders, the poor, the sick, and the imprisoned. Jesus identified himself with the most vulnerable, forsaken, and reviled. The holy cause is found among those in need, and we see God's work reflected in their eyes. The basis of a well-lived life—that is, the judgment of one's life of faith—is whether or not we will have served others by welcoming them at our table and providing sustenance, clothing, and ease to strangers.

In my own life, covenant—both spoken and unspoken—makes a daily impact. As an adult, I live an unspoken covenant with my parents to uphold and to honor their steadfast love for me through my own loving relationships with my husband and children and now grandchildren. My husband has shown me the sacredness of covenant in his steadfastness and undying love, and the love that we share gives meaning to my life. We look forward to our retirement years together as our love and joy of one another continues to grow. The fruits of our love, our children, and now their children, serve as a legacy to the covenant I experienced as a child and as a wife and mother. For these loves of my life, I am eternally grateful and blessed. My life is blessed with the grace of good friends who support me in my daily life and uplift me in my crazy, hectic days. I am confident in my darkest nights that they, along with my family, will be at my side as I tell my story. As Kathleen Norris writes in *The Cloister Walk,* "people in a crisis need to tell their story, from beginning to end, and the best thing—often the only thing—that you can do is to sit there and take it."

Moving along the continuum, I think about my career in academia. At first glance, it is difficult to see where covenant enters into this competitive setting. I made commitments to be a productive academic and to uphold the university's mission. Now, as an academic leader, even in an environment where covenants are not routine, I find it grounding to remember those commitments as I solve problems and form partnerships at the university and in the biotechnology sector. This practice is a constant challenge but it connects my professional practices with a spirit of integrity and right relationship.

In the larger context, I look around our home that we so enjoy, and then the expanse of the earth with its rivers that lap against the river banks and oceans that crash into the shore. It is that never-ending awe of nature, even when it raises its ugly head in destruction, that validates the existence of a mystery that cannot be fully defined. I have a covenant with Mother Earth to embrace the substance of life she has given me freely. I am reminded of Rachel Carson's reverence of the world from *The Sense of Wonder:*

If I had influence with the good fairy who is supposed to preside over the christening of all children I should ask that her gift to each child in the world be a sense of wonder so indestructible that it would last throughout life, as an unfailing antidote against the boredom and disenchantments of later years, the sterile preoccupation with things artificial, the alienation from the sources of our strength.

It is this sense of wonder of the world that stirs the wanderlust in me and my love of travel.

Turning to the church, Unitarian Universalism has also brought me into the intimacy of being human and the ongoing work of cultivating right intention in the world. At church I can seek friendship with others and grow in my understanding of the purpose of my existence. It helps me to live out my faith by constantly calling on me to cutlivate right intention and, most of all, to love. It is the place where I sort out my relationships with others and my relationship to the world.

Our movement and stories are filled with those who did the right thing. We claim people such as Dorothea Dix, Clara Barton, James Reeb, and Theodore Parker—people who listened to that still small voice that we call our conscience. Reeb was a Unitarian Universalist minister, social worker, and civil rights activist. His brutal murder by segregationists while participating in the second Selma to Montgomery march made him one of the martyrs of the American civil rights movement of the 1960s. When Reeb resigned his Presbyterian chaplaincy and applied for Unitarian ministerial fellowship in 1957, he wrote, "I want to participate in the continuous creation of a vision that will inspire our people to noble and courageous living. I want to share actively in the adventure of trying to forge the spiritual ties that will bind mankind together in brotherhood and peace."

In his speech "The Present Aspect of Slavery in America and the Immediate Duty of the North," Theodore Parker, an early Unitarian advocate for abolition, said,

I do not pretend to understand the moral universe; the arc is a long one, my eye reaches but little ways; I cannot calculate the curve and complete the figure by the experience of sight; I can divine it by conscience. And from what I see I am sure it bends towards justice.

Parker's sermon is thought to have inspired Martin Luther King Jr.'s famous assertion in his speech "Where Do We Go From Here?" in which he said, "The arc of the moral universe is long, but it bends towards justice."

Without a covenant that propels us toward something larger than ourselves, we get wedged in the mundane activities of daily existence. Through covenant we uncover something that transforms us.

Social justice work is necessarily bound together with covenant as it helps people respect and hear each other. Being in covenant calls us to listen with intention, communicate honestly in love, and to reflect. It becomes how we are with one another, together in a community of love. In *Who Needs God?* Rabbi Harold Kushner writes, "Emphasis on person-to-person relationships . . . became important in church precisely because it was so rare elsewhere in society. . . . Our place of worship offers us a refuge, an island of caring in the midst of a hostile competitive world."

The concept of covenant evolved over time as a spiritual obligation freely held between persons of a community and between the entire community and the Sacred. One of the powerful rudiments of covenant for Unitarian Universalists is that we make our covenants freely. We choose the commitments we have within our hearts and the promises we make as a community. When we act and identify from the deepest part of ourselves, it becomes easier to take risks; we are less uncertain. As a part of our wider movement, when we act from this place of knowledge and wisdom we make our values tangible in more substantial ways than simply giving to a charity or signing a petition. We heed that still, small voice above all of the other rival voices and withstand the temptation of the shadows in our heart. Our sense of a compelling or holy obligation moves us beyond our church walls and out into the world.

In our country, faith and freedom are intertwined to form a union. The Declaration of Independence, our nation's doctrine, rises above our individual religious requisites, unifying our citizens in a single covenant. Living up to this creed is a constant challenge. In *The American Creed*, Forrest Church eloquently captures the spirit of our American covenant when he writes,

> At our national best, when we wave the American flag or affix red, white and blue ribbons to our lapels, this is not merely an expression of patriotism uniting us against a common foe but rather an emblem of faith uniting us with one another. Our hymns of freedom are sung less in anger than in hope [for our country and for the world we live]. The greatest legacy that America offers . . . is not our devotion to freedom alone but the way in which, at our finest, faith elevates . . . freedom into a sacrament.

Each of us is called to deepen community in different ways, perhaps as an advocate for peace, an activist for justice, or by raising our children in love and compassion. Possibly we are called to lend support to creative thinkers and doers, and perhaps we are called to journey beyond our faith community, even to the far corners of the earth. Covenant is a means to build upon that which we are called to do and how we must be in the world. It is that deliberate step toward what we would like the world to become, weaved into our lives as a holy obligation. We are continually reminded in our covenantal relationships that we live not only in the present but also for strangers and for those who will come after us long after we are gone. Covenant, in its horizontal dimension, should be an unwavering reminder that we, as Unitarian Universalists, do indeed serve something beyond ourselves and that we can only truly live out our values in right relationship with others. It requires us to walk with each other, regardless of our differences.

The Center Must Be Deep

SUSAN M. SMITH

"Thus do we covenant with one another and with God" concludes the popular Unitarian Universalist affirmation arranged by Universalist minister L. Griswold Williams in 1933. It is based on the one written in 1894 by Unitarian minister James Vila Blake which began, "Love is the spirit of this church." This Williams affirmation has undergone literally thousands of rewrites by worship committees deciding what they are willing to promise and whether to include the concluding line, and if so, where to stop. It seems easy to say that we covenant with one another but far more daunting to declare that our covenant is also made with God.

To consider the gravity and the necessity of the promises that we individually and collectively make with the Holy, it is useful to employ the term *God*. However, to use it we must unpack it because this word holds some of the most complex concepts with which humans grapple in relation to the self, the community, and reality itself. We use it when we try to imagine what existed before time and space as we understand it. The twentieth-century Protestant theologian Paul Tillich used the phrase "the Ground of Being" to better express the idea of God. Process theology employs the word *God* to describe both the container for everything that is and the force that entices every next moment to come into existence. This is a considerable departure from the caricature of a bearded and somewhat grumpy old man on high, but even that caricature has held a bit of the truth of what *God* describes.

The first God(s), the God of which our *Homo sapiens* ancestors conceived on the savannahs of Africa some 200,000 years ago, dwelled on mountaintops and spoke through storms and natural beauty and the emotions of the emerging human heart striving to express itself. The grandeur of Mount Kilimanjaro, the infinite depths of the African skies, and the arising of this yearning human heart suggested to these ancestors—as they would to countless human beings through the centuries—that God or the many Gods existed on a plane either literally or figuratively above our own. For this reason, we often speak of God as the vertical dimension of our religious lives while community is the horizontal dimension.

The God of the Hebrew people originated in these same concepts as a force encountered on mountaintops and through natural disasters. But amazingly, this God transformed into a maker of promises, proposing a covenantal relationship that Abraham and Sarah and their descendants were free to enter or to reject. Once entered into this covenant of free will, the parties must ever after maintain it as both obligation and blessing. The relationship of God to the people of the covenant was presented with remarkable parity and as a shared journey where each party would stumble and fall short yet continue to be bound together.

In the Christian scriptures, Jesus of Nazareth went even further in describing God's relationship to the individual as that of a parent to a beloved child. Inspired by this conception of a God who is served by serving "the least" among us, liberation theologians describe God as particularly present among those who are oppressed and suffering and as actually experiencing their suffering. So, this concept of God contains not only the physical and metaphysical but also the intimate and personal. This paradox is expressed in traditional theological language in which God is said to be both transcendent (beyond our realm and our understanding) and immanent (within and among us). We draw upon both these aspects when we consider how we as human beings separately and together enter into covenant with the Holy.

Why bother to employ this term *God* at all? As liberal religion-ists, Unitarian Universalists are comfortable with the co-existence of multiple and differing claims about truth. This tolerance for ambiguity and paradox is the core of liberal religion. In our worship services, we often provide lists of terms that speak of the variety of belief systems among us. We enter into a time of "silence, prayer, *or* meditation" during our "gathering, meeting, *or* worship" and before listening to the "talk, message, *or* sermon." So while it is not strictly necessary to use the term *God* in our intra-faith conversations, we employ it for the sake of clarity in interfaith dialogue with liberal-ists and fundamentalists and all who lie between these poles.

In his landmark book *Stages of Faith: The Psychology of Human Development and the Quest for Meaning,* United Methodist minis-ter and professor James W. Fowler employs a triangle to describe the interplay of the individual, the community, and the Holy in religious life. The base of the triangle is the lateral, covenantal rela-tionship between the individual and the community. Both parties honor and depend on the third and topmost point of the triangle, which Fowler names "centers of value and power." The relationship between the individual and community is a good fit for both of them precisely because they share the particular center of value and power in which they have entrusted their faith. This center may be a shared understanding of God(s), but it can also be any transcendent value such as love, peace, or justice. The community that gathers to honor and serve this value need not be religious in any traditional sense, yet the three necessary components of indi-vidual, community, and center of value and power will be present.

Values worthy of our ultimate allegiance share the para-doxical qualities attributed to God. They are both transcendent and immanent. Love or peace or creative becoming cannot be observed per se. The gathered community can tell stories, sing songs, enact ceremonies, and celebrate holidays about love, but love itself cannot be fully grasped or completely represented. When we say that God is love or that Jesus is the Prince of Peace or that every moment is a moment of creative becoming, we may not have said anything helpful or even intelligible to those who do not share a life-sustaining allegiance to these particular centers of value and power. By the same token, if we can display a value such as wealth or physical beauty then it cannot truly qualify as that upon which we should place our faith. This is what it means to distinguish Gods from idols.

Modern Unitarian Universalism places each congregation in the empowering and awesome position of needing to decide on and be explicit about its shared centers of value and power. It differs in this way from creedal traditions. At the Methodist congregation down the street, they do not say, "We did Jesus last week. What shall we do next?" In the teachings and person of Jesus of Nazareth, the Christian church finds all its highest values and best intentions personified. He is alpha and omega, transcendent and immanent. For two thousand years, the depth of him as a center of value and power has not nearly been exhausted. And this is true for the core of all religions whether it be the Tao, the revelation to Muhammad, or the great pantheon of neopaganism. The center must be deep.

In Unitarian Universalism, we are required to name this core for ourselves. The beginning of all work on mission or vision must begin with an explicit decision about which shared values our particular congregation serves. When our congregation decides on three or four of these transcendent values through a shared discernment process, we can reach much more clarity about our worship, witness, faith development, and vision of beloved community. We will know what we serve and then draw members to us who are self-differentiated, and eager to be placed in service to this vision of the Holy. Since life is transient and ever changing we don't need to, nor should we, carve these values in stone. When we renew the planning cycle in five to seven years, we should again begin with an affirmation of shared transcendent values.

This practice is different from employing themes as a way to unify congregational programming. As noted by Fowler, repetition rather than novelty is the foundation for faith development. This is the reason that religions develop liturgical years made up of seasons, holidays, and observances. These inexhaustible centers of value and power are referenced in the key teaching stories and insights of their traditions annually, with the knowledge that the listeners change as they mature and develop and, having changed, experience the teaching differently every time it is repeated.

Congregational life without the vertical dimension develops an idolatrous focus on our individual and shared happiness. We mistake the community for the transcendent value it should serve and endeavor to be all things to all people for the sake of harmony. However, we must not confuse our bonds with our transcendent values. Many congregations, when asked to identify their most cherished transcendent values, simply cannot imagine anything outside of the horizontal relationship between members and the group. This horizontal dimension is usually described as friendship or family and as acceptance or tolerance.

The individual and community drawn together in service to love, peace, and/or justice have something more than subjective feelings and personal interests by which they are guided. Unitarian Universalist minister and author Forrest Church writes, "God is that which is greater than all and present in each." It is precisely this unity that we acknowledge in our covenantal relationship. Together we are better, stronger, and nobler than we can ever be on our own. Even a rich spiritual life without congregational embodiment can be idolatrous. The just and loving community provides us with accountability and a venue in which we can express our values in tangible acts day by day.

With the addition of transcendent values as part of what is contained in the concept of the Holy, we open possibilities for inspirational and meaningful participation for those who reject all or some concepts of God. We also acknowledge an immense obligation to reach clarity about the value that we share or the God in which we have faith. Only when we know the values or sacred attributes that allow us to rise every day and fight once again the good fight, that comfort us in our darkest hours and to which our grateful hearts turn in exultation, can we begin the work of embodying these values in the world so that they might spread and grow and be more fully manifested. So we align ourselves with these great values and forces when we enter into covenantal life.

Covenants are easy to make and are frequently broken. The real religious practice inherent in a covenantal faith is getting back into covenant when we make mistakes. This is difficult to do when we have disappointed one another or when either an individual member or a congregation has let another down. But the path back into covenant is actually well known because we walk it so often. We make apologies and we accept them. We describe boundaries and expectations and either freely accept them or intentionally reject them. We need liturgies that acknowledge our intention to renew our bonds of community, and also those that restore and reinforce our relationship with whatever we call Sacred and lift our hearts and vision a bit higher.

In our covenants, we acknowledge that we are fallible and sometimes self-serving and also capable of great nobility and self-sacrifice and that it is our intent to be guided by "our better angels." When we consecrate these promises, our words bespeak the best that human beings can imagine for a life bolstered and inspired by the Holy among us, whether we call this the Holy Spirit, the Human Spirit, the Spirit of the Moment, or the Spirits of Love, Peace, and Justice.

EXERCISES

Naming Our Covenants

You will need:

• movable chairs
• newsprint
• journal or paper for each participant
• pens and/or pencils
• markers
• chime or smartphone with gong application
• timekeeping device

Begin by having all participants write out their answers to the following question:

> How would you describe your relationship with the God of your experience?

If participants have no relationship with God, they can write about that.

After writing, divide the group into pairs. Each person tells their partner how they answered the question, perhaps starting out by saying, "It's like . . . " After 5 minutes of one person sharing, the listener shares for 5 minutes. Then they sit together in 10 minutes of silence.

When the leader rings the chime or gong, each partner shares for 5 minutes, answering the following question: What is being faithful to your covenant with your congregation requiring of you now? Then sit together in 10 more minutes of silence, ending with the sound of the chime or gong.

If your group numbers eight or more people, gather in groups of four. Otherwise, gather as a whole group, each person sharing for 5 minutes, answering the following question: What is being faithful requiring of you now? Then, have the group share about the following two questions: How can we be with one another, as we struggle with what is covenantal and liberating? What would allow us to be safe together as emotional, embodied, flawed, and forgiven people? Have one person in each group record the main points.

Reassemble in the whole group. One person from each group names one way we can be together. The leader records these on newsprint.

Leader closes with prayer. Here is one example:

Oh God of our troubled and aspiring lives
Help us to be present to one another as we live in the tensions of our covenants.
Help us to be gracious and loving in hearing the troubles of our friends.
Help us always to express your love in our lives.
In the name of all that is Holy we pray. Amen.

Journaling

What is being faithful asking of me?

FIVE

Faithfulness

Transcending boundaries is hard work. For one thing, I've created more of them since I was young, and I've built them higher and stronger than they once were. For another thing, I'm much more self-righteous and much less humble than I was then. Sometimes, when I am at my best, I remember that the "other" I distinguish myself from could be me in another time, another place, another circumstance. Then, I remember the words of a colleague who observed that it is "my racism, my sexism, my homophobia" that I am called upon to address. So, I take a few deep breaths and begin to release the fears that are the boundaries between me and my fellow humans.

—Yvonne Seon, "Transcending Boundaries"

Introduction

By being faithful we are introduced to new possibilities. Our souls grow by crossing boundaries and experiencing the ways we belong to the stranger and they belong to us. We rely on deep sources of strength as we practice confession, forgiveness, reparation, and reconciliation. Through faithfulness we repair ourselves and heal the world.

Love Says the Answer Is Yes

SUZELLE LYNCH

In 1963, Martin Luther King Jr. stood on the steps of the Lincoln Memorial in Washington, D.C., during the Great March for Jobs and Freedom and spoke a powerful dream. One day the children of former slaves and former slave owners would sit down together at the table of brotherhood. One day all of our children would be judged not by the color of their skin, but by the content of their character. One day our nation would rise up and live out the self-evident truth that all of us are created equal. More than 250,000 people gathered to hear him; millions more listened via radio or television, including my parents.

My parents, like so many white Unitarian Universalists, loved King. They loved his dream. I think they longed to live in what might be called a "rainbow world," a world where people of all races and ethnicities and national origins live, work, play, and worship together in peace and joy. The rainbow world is a world where there is justice and equity for all people: where race, class, age, education, ability or disability, immigration status, religion, sexual orientation, gender identity, and gender expression are not barriers to equal participation and productivity in all areas of life. I was raised on a middle-class, European-American interpretation of King's dream: that "color-blindness" and personal non-prejudice (with help from affirmative action and programs such as Head Start) would make this rainbow world possible. I was raised to believe that we Unitarian Universalists, called to affirm that every person is a child of God with inherent worth and dignity, could help make it possible.

This year I visited the Lincoln Memorial with my husband and our teenage daughter. We stood in the place where King spoke. As we gazed out toward the Washington Monument, a rainbow world crowd swirled around us: people of all ages and many races, speaking many languages; children laughing and jumping on the stark white marble steps; older folks looking up reverently at the huge statue of Lincoln; teens snapping smart phone pictures or texting, heads down, oblivious of the activity around them. We marveled at the crowd's diversity, and then moved on, walking farther down the Mall to the Korean War Memorial.

As we approached that memorial, two pale gray, life-size statues of American soldiers came into view. I stopped in my tracks. "Ghosts," I blurted out. "They're ghosts." The soldiers' flowing rain ponchos draped over their heavy backpacks and seemed to flap in an invisible wind as the soldiers struggled up a slope covered with dense brush. They leaned forward, separated from one another by the shrubbery, their faces marked with fear and misery.

On a black marble slab at the top of the memorial we read these words: "Our nation honors her sons and daughters who answered the call to defend a country they never knew and a people they never met." As I read those words, tears began to run down my cheeks. Suddenly it struck me that without this war, this bloody, hard-to-understand war that no one had taught me about in school, the two people I love most in all the world would never have been born. I fell into my husband's arms and started to sob.

I met my husband, Young Kim, at a planning meeting for a Unitarian Universalist young adult ministry conference in 1991. He walked in the door of our mutual friend's house where the meeting took place, saw me standing in the kitchen cutting up oranges, and did a double take. My features clearly said "white girl," but my dark tan skin said something else. What was I? Greek, maybe? In my own head, a similar conversation: He looked Asian, but I'd never met an Asian guy so tall and broad shouldered. What was he? After the meeting we went to the beach with some of the other young adults, and Young told me about himself. His parents came to the United States for college after the Korean War. They met here, married, and stayed—settling in the Deep South where Young was born. I found his background very interesting, but in my color-blind way it never occurred to me to tell him about mine. He was "the other"; his life needed explaining, not mine.

Young reached out across a border to meet me that day, but I didn't know it. Lifelong experience with white people who asked, "Where are you from?" with a particular lilt in their voices taught him that I, too, must be wondering. But there was more to it than that. If I was to know who he was on the inside, he knew he had to help me see who he was on the outside. Later in our life together we'd paraphrase Audre Lorde as our shorthand for this—she said, "Don't focus on the fact that I'm black and lesbian, but don't forget about it, either." His "otherness" was not something to be ignored or transcended; it was part of his giftedness. Lorde also writes, "It is not our differences that divide us. It is our inability to recognize, accept, and celebrate those differences."

What do I mean when I say Young crossed a border? Unitarian Universalist Association President Peter Morales put it this way: "We UUs often lament that, despite our advocacy of multiculturalism and anti-racism, ours remains a faith that is largely middle-class and Eurocentric. Our world, meanwhile, is rapidly becoming more diverse. In the United States, people of European descent will be in the minority in a generation or so. . . . Our challenge is to reach beyond the confines of our personal social and cultural experience . . . [we must learn] to cross . . . the borders of race, culture, and social class." On the day we met, Young took the risk of telling me who he was.

Morales challenges those of us who are white, dominant-culture people to get out into the world and cross borders. To build the world we long for, we not only need to continue our antiracism, anti-oppression work but we also have to escape the confines of our comfort zones and cross into a neighborhood or a culture different from our own. Morales asks us to become aware of our own feelings as we do so. Do we feel afraid—and how does fear shape our actions? Do we approach persons who are different from us with unconscious arrogance, expecting them to accept us on our terms? Or do we approach with humility, feeling our way along to find out what their terms might be? When we cross a border, who is "the other"?

When we met, my husband was accustomed to crossing borders. Non-dominant-culture people learn early in life to navigate in more than one cultural world; it's a survival skill. Knowing one's own identity is like a passport—it provides a sense of grounding as we step over the border into the unknown. When we know who we are, we can adapt our behavior to function well in a new cultural context without losing our souls. As our love for one another grew, Young's clarity about his identity challenged me to see myself more fully. As I began to explore my ethnicity, culture, and class, my whiteness took on new colors. The lens through which I view the world began to become visible to me. I began to see and to love my own otherness.

I am Irish, English, French, and Finnish—with a little German mixed in somewhere. Some of my father's ancestors arrived during the American Revolution, and his family has been middle class for generations. My mother's people came later and lived closer to the land. I'm named for my mother's grandmother, Sanna Kaisa Wirtanen, who emigrated from Finland to the Upper Peninsula of Michigan in 1916. She brought my grandmother, ten-year-old Elna, with her. They came to join Jaako, Sanna Kaisa's husband, on a cooperative farm.

Jacob and Susanna, as they became known in this country, worked hard on the farm. My grandmother Elna fled their way of life as soon as she came of age. She moved downstate, and by marrying a manager in an automobile factory she charged across the boundary between working-class life and the middle-class milieu. This move challenged her family's understanding.

My own marriage was unexpectedly challenging for my mother. When I first told her I'd fallen in love with a wonderful Korean-American man, she snapped, "My brother died in the Korean War!" It was true. Jimmy, my mother's darling little brother, the person she loved most in all the world, was killed along with thousands of other soldiers in the Battle of Chosin Reservoir. His body was never recovered and she was devastated. It took me years to realize that with my marriage I dragged my mother over a border she was not ready to cross. Only in another lifetime could she have embraced my husband and daughter as gifts her brother's sacrifice made possible. Only in another lifetime would she have been able to see the poetic justice of my beautiful family. Today I am simply grateful that she loved and accepted us as well as she could. It was beautiful, and it was enough.

My parents had a deeply humanist Unitarian Universalist faith. Yet when I look back at my upbringing, I see the Holy ever present in their love for me and in the love I felt from others in the small, lay-led UU fellowship to which we belonged. God was a larger Love holding us all, present in our relationships with one another and with all living things, reminding us that we belonged to each other, calling us to ever-greater hospitality, responsibility, and joy.

That larger Love is what calls us to cross borders. It's a love we need to be guided by, a love that recognizes all people as beings who are as blessed and beloved as we are. This Love allows us to see that other people's stories and habits and ways of work and worship are just as important and "normal" as ours are. It reminds us that we are all the other; we are all the stranger, the guest—but we can also be the host, the neighbor, the beloved.

There are so many ways to practice crossing borders. My congregation sends teams of volunteers to Nicaragua where they live and work side by side with people whose lives are rich with love and community as well as marked by startling material poverty. These volunteers go with experienced guides who help them navigate cultural differences and integrate what they are learning, so that they return with eyes opened to parts of their own culture that they took for granted and hearts opened in an expanded understanding of who "we" are—of who's part of our family. Closer to home, our Habitat for Humanity team crosses borders regularly when they go out to help spruce up and repair homes in downtrodden neighborhoods. My congregation is beginning to understand that crossing borders is a way to practice their faith, equip themselves to help shape a world of love and justice, and to grow the soul of our church.

Crossing borders isn't always easy, of course. I've learned this again and again during the ten years I have lived in metropolitan Milwaukee, Wisconsin. Generations of legal and de facto segregation and discrimination here have worn a deep trench of mistrust between people of different races, cultures, and classes. Thus, no matter how full of good intentions and integrity I am, someone from across the racial or class border probably has good reason to judge me as just another privileged, pushy white woman. And of course, I wrestle with my own visible and unconscious prejudices and stereotypes.

In recent years I've been humbled and changed by an ongoing border-crossing experience. Two years ago, desperate to get back into a healthy exercise habit, I joined the last remaining Milwaukee-area outlet of a women's workout club that features the kind of exercise I love. The club is located two miles east across the invisible border that divides my suburban turf from the city of Milwaukee; it's in a "rough" neighborhood. But the club itself is far from rough—it's a place of great kindness and joy. Sherri, the owner, has created a respectful and empowering environment in which women of all ages and all body sizes can exercise together.

You'll notice that I said women of "all ages and body sizes," not "all races and cultures." That's because I seem to be the only white European-American club member. In two years there I've met two Latina women; everybody else is African American.

I noticed this right away, and I worried about it. Would the women there accept me? Was I, the white girl, invading a place that was safe and nurturing for black women and messing it up? Should I ask Sherri if it was all right for me to be there? Or was it stupid and racist of me to even think of bringing it up? Crossing borders can make one terribly self-conscious.

When I first joined the club, nobody talked to me unless Sherri introduced us and started the conversation. It's so uncomfortable being the white stranger in a room full of African-American women exercising, laughing, and talking together—ignoring you. I struggled against projecting my discomfort outward, struggled against assuming there was something wrong with "them." I just kept going back, week after week, month after month, and gradually I came to know people there. Gradually I came to be known there as well.

Nowadays, it's a privilege to hear the joys and struggles of the women at the club and to share some of my own. I've uncovered and let go of so many assumptions about class, one by one. I've learned to listen more than I speak. And I've learned that white power and privilege do not disappear just because someone trusts me.

There have been some awkward moments, like the time when a close relative of one of the staff members died, and folks were collecting money for her. Wanting to fit in with the group and support this nice staff member, I opened my wallet and pulled out a $20 bill. "Will this do?" I asked. Then I noticed that others were contributing just a dollar or two. I felt so stupid. The collection was a symbol of support, not an act of "help." It would have made things worse to make change from the pile of bills inside the sympathy card, so I quietly tucked in the $20 and signed my name. The next time I would know what to do.

What I didn't know was that the next time the sympathy card would be for me.

My mom died in March 2012. One morning not long after that, I found an envelope with my name on it on the club's check-in counter. Inside there was a tidy pile of one and five dollar bills and a wealth of sympathy and prayers. The love in that card was such balm for my grieving heart. I keep it close as a reminder that even though the women at my workout club and I could be "others" to one another, we belong to each other. Will learning to cross borders lead us to the rainbow world? Will it lead to a world in which we can all belong to each other? Will it lead to the realization of King's dream? Love tells me the answer is yes. If we cross borders with open hearts, holding out before us our vulnerability, not just our curiosity, the answer will be yes. If we will begin to see how our own culture shapes our experiences of "the other," if we will let go of our way as the norm for all human being and doing and embrace our own otherness— the answer will be yes. Will it take time and spiritual discipline? Yes. It is work we do for ourselves, but even more for our children and their children. If we desire a world of wholeness, a world where each person is truly seen, accepted, and celebrated, a world of love and justice—we must follow Love's call now.

The Amazing Grace of Each Other

JENNY WEIL

I came to Unitarian Universalism during a time of loss and confusion and found welcome. Church and faith were the shore after the shipwreck. But comfort alone didn't change my life—it was the call to community and covenant, accountability and interdependence that enlarged my sense of possibility and deepened my capacity to love and be loved. I have greater peace, strength, and purpose because I've come to know myself and others as necessary (and necessarily imperfect) parts of an interdependent whole. This is a story of how I was saved by faith and belonging, and how church became an essential place to practice living my part in the family of things.

Wretchedness

Years ago, on one of my earliest visits to a Unitarian Universalist church, I was surprised to hear the congregation sing "Amazing grace! How sweet the sound, that saved a soul like me." Where's the "wretch"? I wondered, and later asked my friend, a longtime Unitarian Universalist. She assured me, emphatically, that there are no wretches in Unitarian Universalism. She delivered this as good news, if not the Good News, but I wasn't so sure.

Like so many others, I'd come to church in crisis. I was twenty-nine years old and six months pregnant. My marriage was ending, messily. Heartbroken, but hoping to provide a peaceful, stable start for our baby, I'd moved in with my parents in Dallas, Texas, leaving behind job, friends, and cultural affinity in Cambridge, Massachusetts. When I'd been home for about a month, I was mugged. Out walking early one evening, I was jumped and beaten by a young man, a boy really, in a pressed button-down shirt and khakis. He seemed almost as startled to throw punches as I was to receive them. He wanted my bag, but it crossed my body over one shoulder and he was too frantic to see that by forcing me back, he only increased tension on the strap. He seemed afraid—the police later speculated that this was a gang initiation requirement—and it might have been my own fear as much as any physical trauma that sent me into labor. I doubled over. The bag came loose; he ran off with it. All the while, cars passed without stopping. Maybe those drivers were startled, too. Street crime is all but unheard of in my parents' neighborhood. With no help coming, I made the short walk home in a daze. Emergency room doctors stopped the labor and I was home by morning, bruised but not badly hurt. The stolen bag contained only a journal and pen. As crimes go, it was both unlikely and trivial, but it made for a disheartening culmination to a sad season.

And so it was that on the Sunday morning we sang—and argued about—"Amazing Grace," I was living with my parents, a pregnant, divorcing twenty-nine-year-old recent victim of an improbable and pointless crime. I was having trouble telling insult from injury. Little wonder that my friend should insist upon a fundamental tenet of Unitarian Universalism: that all are welcomed, worthy, and loved, just as we are. Easy to say, I thought, but at that moment, I knew with equal conviction that it wasn't true. I wasn't good. Despite the tender attentions of friends and family, I felt neither loved nor lovable. I'd failed at my marriage, and my child would be born to a broke and broken single mother. It's not that I didn't recognize my self-pity. I wanted to pull myself together, but my self-loathing was a riptide I lacked the will and strength to out-swim. With no sense of contradiction, I also knew that my soon-to-be ex-husband was neither good nor lovable—he was responsible! I had evidence! Alternately dismayed and disgusted, I knew one thing for sure: someone was a wretch in this situation. And what of the mugging? Only a hopeless culture could produce this kind of violence, indifference, and waste. It seemed to me at the time that the best that could be said of a faith that would embrace any of us, let alone all of us, was that it lacked discretion. Maybe it also offered cheap grace.

Welcome

One thing about church is that they'll take you in when you feel unfit for human company, even if you intend to sit suspicious and cross-armed in the back. I returned to my friend's church, slipping in and out of services with little in mind but my own need for encouragement. But church life pulls against such isolation, reminding us how the world moves: babies are born and dedicated, couples marry and split, people get sick and get better. Or they don't. We are continually reminded that suffering and good fortune come to us all, the best and worst of us. The best and worst are needed, too, for so much celebrating and commiserating, serving and praying, organizing and demonstrating, teaching and learning. In its quiet way, church began to relieve my burden of specialness—in the suffering I felt and the suffering I caused. At the same time, I came to feel that my particular gifts were not just needed, but discovered and recognized at church. Engaging in community where we share vulnerability as well as joy called me back to perspective and participation in the larger world. Incredibly, my friend had been right: I'd been received with dignity and put to use.

Confession

Before long, I felt it necessary to schedule a meeting with the minister. Glad as I was to feel a part of things at church, I thought she ought to know that I was not a spiritual person. I was too angry. I felt cut off from any possible notion of God and all the nice religious people in the congregation. The truth tumbled out: not just my furious resentments, but also the case I made against myself. By the time I was done, an awful lot of pain and ugliness lay on the table between us. My minister listened and nodded compassionately, but when she spoke, she was matter of fact. She said that anger was, in fact, my current spiritual state, and that would have to be okay. Perhaps I might consider how my anger might serve. We talked some more about fear and sadness and grief, but the message was the same: I could set my burden down. Nothing I felt or did was unspeakable; she could bear to hear it, and it did not come between us. Once I let go of the shame of the unspeakable, I could begin to make peace and make amends.

In the years since that conversation, I've thought a lot about the gifts of confession: we are all, paradoxically, better and worse than we think; our failings needn't disqualify us from community, and there is no shame in asking for forgiveness. In fact, we do well to ask for it regularly, lest our burden accumulate. We will sin again.

Forgiveness

In his essay "Adolescence and the Stewardship of Pain," writer and Christian theologian Frederick Buechner speaks of the need to be "good stewards of our pain." We ought to take care, he says, how we cultivate our narratives of pain and what meaning and use we make of our experience. It's a valid warning and invitation. It can be tempting, Buechner notes, to deny our pain out of shame or longing for invulnerability. Or minimize it in false virtue, comparing it dismissively to the suffering of others. At the other extreme, he warns against becoming like Dickens's Miss Havisham, bitterly, obsessively curating mementos of life's most anguished moments. Pain misused, he suggests, alienates and spreads. Pain well used can open our hearts and teach us something about how to live.

This has been my experience. Understood in isolation, it's easy to cultivate indignation, self-pity, or shame over losses and slights, but understood in the context of community, other meanings become possible. Remembering my own suffering, I am spurred to act compassionately. Remembering the suffering I myself have caused, I practice righting my relationships, giving and receiving forgiveness more freely precisely because our faith affirms my goodness even in the face of my imperfection. In community, too, we can see patterns, urging us toward questions of justice and responsibility.

Most of us feel compelled to make meaning of the big events that rock and shape our lives, but my experience of church is that even my petty grievances—ones for which meanings spring up all too reflexively—are rewritten as moments of continuity and connection. My weekly drive to church, for example: Beyond all reason, I harry myself about arriving on time. Judgments of others come fast and furious: your gas-guzzling SUV, your selfish double-parking, your reckless distracted driving. At my worst, I'm inclined to agree with comedian George Carlin: Everyone who drives slower than I do is an idiot; everyone who drives faster is a maniac. If I am not careful, I arrive for worship exhausted and hostile. But, in the church parking lot, I gladly wait while a joyful, boisterous extended family piles out of that SUV. I watch that poor parking job as it happens and notice that the driver is a man distracted by grief over the recent loss of his partner. A few minutes later, warmly ensconced among my church family, it's easier to recognize and release my self-absorption at being inconvenienced on the road. It isn't that there's not a conversation to be had about the environment or road safety; it's that the context has shifted from alienation to interdependence. By the time we join our voices in song, we are more than a collection of individuals. Something holy transpires and we transcend ourselves. It's humbling and freeing to be so regularly and easily reunited with humanity in the need to forgive and be forgiven.

Covenant and Reconciliation

For several years, I attended church without joining. I loved my UU church; I also found it wanting. I recall telling a visiting consultant that our church ought to be friendlier, more welcoming. About this time, I became engaged to a man I'd been dating. As we discussed marriage, he asked about which church we would join. Balking at two big commitments at once—church membership and marriage—I resisted, but when I came to understand his determination on this point, I relented. We joined the UU church, and this as much as anything else occasioned a small but life-changing epiphany: We, the congregation, are the church. If "church" needed to be friendlier, I would have to offer my hand in coffee hour. How much of the welcome I received I had taken for granted. How easily I default to an atomized narrative about how I encounter the world, when in fact there is a truthful and more promising story about how we, together, create the word, our lives defining and testifying to the possibilities.

Belonging to our church has been a blessing, unconditional in the love it offers, but demanding in the way of all meaningful relationships. Like marriage, like parenting, belonging to church has been a liberating constraint. We have chosen this place and these people, and our lives and values can be measured by the quality of our commitment. Our covenant means that we're willing to be transformed by one another and to be accountable for our effect on others. We have thrown in our lot together. That means, among other things, that I must forgo the pleasure of smirking at a distance and undertake to understand outlying points of view in the congregation. It means that I need to love (or at least make peace with) the cranks and glad-handers, those I find too eccentric or too conventional, just as they try to make peace with me. Even if we never achieve more than the detente of the doughnut table, we remain connected. It means that when I fail to live up to community ideals—whether I am called out or not—I must keep showing up, owning up, and trying again. In return, I am free of feeling adrift or alone in this life. I'm needed at church, as we all are. We have work to do in the world. Not as we might be in some better version of ourselves, but now. Our differences are real. We can hurt one another. But together, we can be good. We can be love.

Today, my son is seventeen. His father, stepfather, and I are reconciled in gratitude for our son and partnership as his family. A tiny scar on my lip reminds me of the night when I grappled with someone else's son, just as young and full of possibility. We were both afraid, I think, and certainly both at risk. I hope the years since have been as merciful to him as they've been to me. I hope he has found his way.

Church has become my way. It's where I practice recognition of what is already true: that we are bound to one another, and by that understanding, we might be saved. This is how church life heals. It is grace enough. It is amazing.

EXERCISES

Faithful Connections

You will need:
- movable chairs
- chime or smartphone with gong application
- timekeeping device

Divide the group into pairs. Have each person share with their partner their answers to the following questions. After 10 minutes, the leader will ring the chime or gong, indicating that it is time for the speaker and listener to swap roles.

- Give a brief example of how you tell your story as if you are an isolated individual.
- Give a brief example of how you could tell your story in a different way.
- Have you ever prayed for creative discomfort, as a way to pay attention to "otherness"?
- What might become possible with this practice?

After 10 minutes, the leader will ring the chime or gong. Gather again as a large group. Share with one another some of the highlights of your one-on-one conversations.

Journaling

Write down experiences you have this month of "liberating constraint."

SIX

Discernment

My eyes already touch the sunny hill,
going far ahead of the road I have begun.
So we are grasped by what we cannot grasp;
it has its inner light, even from a distance—

and changes us, even if we do not reach it,
into something else, which hardly sensing it, we already are;
a gesture waves us on, answering our own wave . . .
but what we feel is the wind in our faces.

—Rainer Maria Rilke, "A Walk"

Introduction

Discernment is much more than using good judgment about matters of importance. It is also a quality of wisdom and a way of living our whole lives, in authenticity, in covenant with others and with the Holy. It is the capacity for connecting our decisions to our deepest calling and purpose. Speaking about the movement of the spirit in our lives with people we trust enhances the power of discernment. The life of the spirit is not just found in us but also among us. The practice of deep listening, asking clarifying questions, and praying for one another keep us faithful to whose we are.

Spiritual But Not Private

DOUGLAS TAYLOR

"Why are you restless?" she asked.

I was in a small circle of colleagues talking about the movement of the spirit in my life. Each of us in the group had been asked to reflect on this topic. One person would speak, we would sit in silence, then ask clarifying questions, sit together in silence again, and then we would pray. It was a comfortable, slow pace of listening, speaking, and silence.

When it was my turn to share, I spent my five minutes talking about my desire for more prayer, more open-hearted communal experiences in my faith community. I talked about my yearning to offer more of my authentic self and to help shape opportunities for others in the community I serve to do the same. Seeing those as broad and vague statements, I tried to be more specific. "I am good at leading that traditional model of Sunday UU worship. I value it and don't want to abandon it," I explained. "I just feel a yearning to something more: more energy, more life, more gratitude." One aspect of doing so is for us to open up, to be vulnerable, to risk. What I expressed to the group may not have been a significant risk, but it seemed so at the time.

The first clarifying question came: "Why are you restless?" In some way, I had given the impression that I am restless. Why am I restless? Am I restless? Somehow this question cracked me open. Her question refocused my reflection and shifted my vision.

I offered some response, but I do not now recall what I said. I do remember the question. And more, I remember the experience of being opened by the shared process. After one or two more clarifying questions we returned to silence before praying and then turning our focus to the next person in the circle.

This was my first experience of a discernment group. It gave me an opportunity to reflect on my calling, the movement of the spirit, the presence of God, the yearnings of my soul. But more than that: it was a conversation out loud rather than just my private musings. I've asked myself these sorts of questions before, but it was a rare gift to speak about it out loud with colleagues who helped me take it seriously and explore the implications. There is something truly transformative about trusting the process of a group to allow truth and the promptings of the spirit to emerge.

Discernment is about choosing the right path or the good path for your life. The word *discernment* has a Latin origin: *dis,* apart, and *cernere,* to sift. And so: to separate by sifting. Its synonym, *discrimination*, carries a negative and pejorative connotation. But when two roads diverge in a yellow wood, you need to make a choice; you need to discriminate between the two options and choose one.

Quakers call such groups "clearness committees." Buddhists might see a group like this as parallel to the *sangha*, which helps members follow the Eightfold Path. Orthodox Christians and Catholics consider such groups as part of the process of spiritual direction. Taoists endeavor to follow the Tao, the right path, which may be the closest Eastern religious equivalent to Western spiritual discernment. Faith traditions have various structures and formulas to help adherents know how to choose well and how to live well. What might an authentically Unitarian Universalist perspective offer for discernment? How do we do this?

At our theological core, Unitarian Universalism has long held fast to the freedom of conscience. The chief organizing concept for Unitarian Universalism is our deep commitment to individual experience and reason as the arbiter of truth and meaning. As Unitarian Universalists we do not gather around a doctrine or creed; rather, we join in a pledge to help each other search for what is ultimately meaningful in life. We do not rely on church authorities or scripture or the long-held traditions of our people to serve as the backdrop of discernment. Other religious traditions will look to such sources for guidance. But when we long to know if the choice we would make is wise, we do not check with church doctrine or ask, "What would Emerson do?" Instead, we discern meaning and truth through the use of reason and a reliance on personal experience.

This is very individualistic; it seems very private. But the deeper story of how it works reveals a context that is more communal than it might seem at first. We are individualistic. But we come together in community through covenant. The binding element of our communities is our promise of how we will be together. This context of covenant contains our commitment to the freedom of conscience. Covenant is communal; thus, there we have an abiding tension between the individual and the community.

We are certainly not alone in this tension. The contemporary understanding of spirituality is that it is something private and personal. People say they are "spiritual but not religious," often meaning that they don't bother with the organized, communal aspect of religion. Certainly the bulk of spirituality is caught up in the private experience of an individual's practice. And contrariwise, religion has a lot of social and publically prophetic aspects that are significant. But the phrase "spiritual but not religious" is deceptive implying that spirituality is private and religion is public.

A discernment group is certainly spiritual but it is not private. The communal aspect is a key piece of the discernment work. It is too easy to go off into a corner and think our private deep thoughts without checking in with others. It is too easy to drift toward the danger of giving unchecked reign to every ego whim we think up masquerading as the movement of the spirit. A discernment group grounds us in openness, trust, and humility.

Consider the experience of St. Teresa of Avila, a Christian nun from the 1500s who founded the Discalced Carmelite sisters. She is known for having ecstatic visions of Jesus Christ. She was warned against such visions and told by church authorities that they were diabolical in origin, temptations to lure her away from the truth. But others close to her helped her to discern them as true visions. The evidence of her life suggests she was right to trust the visions. She is remembered as a mystic, saint, and reformer of the Carmelite order. But how did she know she could trust her visions? How did she decide?

To bring this question to our context, how can we trust our sense of things and what our calling is? Emerson tells us to trust our own experience. But we know all too well that we can get caught between our ego and our self-doubt. Should we trust our uncertainty about our calling? Or should we trust the rush of feeling that comes with being the center of attention? We can reason our way around in circles.

All the great spiritual luminaries and wise teachers who suggested we seek silence and solitary time to listen deeply to our inner lives were right. The deeply interior and private aspects of spirituality are the key to spiritual maturity. But none of the wise souls and mystics and great teachers suggested that by tamping down the noise and fret of the crowd we bind ourselves to the whims and wiles of our willful egos and anxieties. Indeed, that is exactly what, with fierce humble effort, they suggest we grapple against. Most of those luminaries and teachers of the past were members of a monastic or intentional community. The depth of spiritual discernment for such people arose from the context of their regular interactions with others. One great benefit of having a group around us is to double check our spiritual progress against what others see of our lives.

We can use the analogy of eyesight. We can perceive depth because we have two eyes. My single perspective can show me truth, but a second perspective allows me to evaluate—to discern —the information I have gleaned from my single point of view. Or let us consider the analogy of hot coals. Seventeenth-century Quaker Isaac Pennington describes a spiritual gathering in his day with these words: "They are like a heap of fresh and living coals, warming one another as a great strength, freshness, and vigor of life flows into all."

Consider the changing landscape of your life. If you are feeling lost or caught or unbalanced or stuck, then spending time in discernment with others will help. Ask yourself: What do I need to be doing? Where is my joy and how am I giving joy to others? What is at the root of my restlessness? Listen for answers in yourself, but listen also to the answers from others; they may see in you what you might not always see in yourself. When we speak openly about the movement of the Spirit in our lives, when we speak about it out loud with others in an intentional group, we experience a shift in our vision and perspective.

In his book *Discernment: The Art of Choosing Well,* Pierre Wolff shares a reflection a friend offered of the experience of a mature discernment group. It is similar to comments I have heard from members of the discernment group we've had in our congregation over the past two years.

> Choosing community life, I thought that decisions would be easier; in fact thanks to my respectful companions, I was invited to assume responsibility for myself at deeper and deeper levels. It was awful to be treated not as a baby, but rather as an adult by people who did not act as mothers, fathers, guardians or judges, but as my true brothers and sisters . . . it was awful but beautiful. I felt my dignity.

A good group will involve a lot of appreciative listening. What we want in such a group are people who will take time to consider where the life-giving openings might be in the experience. We need the courage to set aside societal expectations as well as our egos to allow the spirit room to breathe through us. When a conversation like this happens among us, it opens all the participants to a deeper level of experience.

Through this process the community as well as the individual deepens and grows in spiritual maturity. The variety of conversations enlarges and the tone of those conversations grows in maturity as well. A congregation that makes space for its members to speak with each other about the depth of meaning and the movement of the spirit in their lives is a congregation that can hold intimate and ultimate questions—not an easy accomplishment given the culture we live in. Through this process the community can honor, respectfully challenge, and encourage a diversity of beliefs and values.

I think of the process our congregation used to create our current mission statement. We began with telling each other our stories about a time when we felt the movement of the spirit in our lives. We didn't use that phrase exactly. We asked each other, "Tell me of a time of transcendence in your personal experience." From those stories we lifted up the values we hold as individuals and the values we hold as a congregation. In the personal stories we told each other, we uncovered our values of compassion, justice, connection, acceptance, and freedom. In other words, the movement of the spirit is felt in times of compassion, justice, connection, acceptance, and freedom according to the gathering of Unitarian Universalists in this congregation.

We learned through that process the power of shared vision through discernment. We learned that what I hold most dear is not exactly the same as what the person next to me holds most dear, but we can still make room for each other. We learned that the way the spirit moves in my life is not the same as the way the spirit moves in the next person's life, but that we are part of a congregation where the spirit moves in such a way that we both are nourished in this community.

The work of discernment in a Unitarian Universalist community is the work of opening and listening. We open and listen to the "still small voice within" as well as to the voices of others around us for guidance and support. We open and listen not only for our own needs and desires but also for the needs and desires of the community and the other people with us on this beloved journey. We open and listen for the spirit of life and love that can lead us.

A solid Unitarian Universalist practice of discernment begins with an abiding respect for the freedom of conscience, the respect for each person's capacity to seek out truth and meaning. But a deep aspect of this is a communal practice as well, held in covenant and in trust. A discernment group is a place where we can speak and be heard and discover the unfolding movement of the spirit in our lives.

Down the Mountain

JEN CROW

When I was a teenager, I dreamed of living alone in a small, sparse hermitage somewhere far out of the way. My hut would be tucked into the side of a hill, kind of like a hobbit house, and I would live there alone, eating mushrooms I'd found in the nearby forest. I'd read and meditate and pray, I'd write poetry and deep spiritual works there in the solitude. It would be great.

There were, however, a few big problems with this scenario. For starters, I was sixteen. It wasn't legal to live alone in the woods and as much as I would have disagreed with this at the time, I really hadn't had enough life experience yet to claim wisdom. It also dawned on me, after awhile, that not many people have a use for spiritual truths developed in solitude. After all, how would they work when the rubber met the road and we had to emerge from our hermitage in the woods?

It turned out that the woods and that little hobbit house tucked in the side of the hill are great for renewal and reflection for me. They are wonderful as a retreat and a respite, a place to nourish my soul and repair my spirit. But hope as I might they aren't the place where I could—or would—live.

Looking back, it's no surprise that solitude seemed like the essential ingredient of spiritual development. In so much of the writing and thinking out there about spirituality, the spiritual path is understood to be solitary. While we may gather in groups for instruction and encouragement, ultimately the path must be walked alone. From ancient times to the present day, we see it. The holy ones lock themselves away in monasteries or travel alone on long journeys. They meditate for days, submerge themselves in study, go off on a solitary odyssey, or sit quietly in prayer. Some sit under the Bodhi tree while others wander the desert—and so often whatever shape the holy ones' spiritual journey takes, it takes them there alone.

In a culture that encourages us to spend more and more time alone, the lure of the solitary spiritual journey can be strong. In their book *The Lonely American,* psychiatrists Jacqueline Olds and Richard Schwartz describe a simultaneous push and pull that seems to be driving Americans further apart from one another. "The push," they say, "is the increasing franticness of daily life, which makes one want to step back whenever possible to reduce the deafening background noise. The pull is the American ideal of the self-reliant loner-hero, which can make stepping back feel like a badge of superiority." The sad result of this simultaneous push and pull is that more and more of us are stepping back from each other, finding ourselves lonely and disconnected in the midst of one of the most highly technologically connected societies in the world.

A recent study found that 25 percent of the people surveyed did not have a single person in their lives with whom they discussed matters of importance. Some people did not have a single person to talk to. The U.S. Census of 2000 showed that more people live alone today than at any other point in American history. And we're moving farther and farther away from each other, too, whether it is across the country or into the isolation of our own homes or rooms, complete with our own TVs and phones and cars to preserve our peace.

As we move farther apart from one another, whether physically or emotionally, we become a nation of socially disconnected people. We become people who have a terribly hard time listening to ourselves and each other, and we suffer physically, emotionally, and spiritually as a result. Mother Teresa once remarked that

America is one of the poorest cultures in the world. She noticed a spiritual poverty here—a lack of connection and meaning that pervades our nation.

In this culture, it makes sense that we have moved toward an individualized idea of spirituality. Within our context of disconnection, many have turned solely to solitary spirituality and spiritual practices. But an isolated spirituality, a spirituality of retreat only, cannot last for long. The Buddha got up from under the tree; Thoreau rejoined society; Jesus emerged again from his time in the wilderness, rejoining his disciples and walking straight into the heart of the city. My own experience, and the teachings of our greatest prophets tell us this truth: Solitary spiritual practice works best for most of us when paired with a communal experience. The great theologian Dietrich Bonhoeffer once said, "Let the person who cannot be alone beware of community. Let the person who is not in community beware of being alone."

While solitary spiritual practices can quiet the mind and help us to hear the still small voice within, they will also bring us right back into community with each other if we practice them with heart and integrity. When we sit alone in prayer or mediation, read the great teachers, walk, or do yoga, our hearts open and soften; we can achieve clarification, discernment, and communion with that which is larger than ourselves, calling us back to this world, to compassion and kindness in all that we do.

In her book *Comfortable with Uncertainty,* Buddhist teacher Pema Chödrön puts it this way:

> Spiritual awakening is frequently described as a journey to the top of a mountain. We leave our attachments and our worldliness behind and slowly make our way to the top. At the peak we have transcended all pain. The only problem with this metaphor is that we leave all others behind. . . . On the journey of the warrior-boddhisattva, the path goes down, not up, as if the mountain pointed toward the earth instead of the sky. Instead of transcending the suffering of

all creatures, we move toward turbulence and doubt however we can. We explore the reality and unpredictability of insecurity and pain, and we try not to push it away. If it takes years, if it takes lifetimes, we let it be as it is. At our own pace, without speed or aggression, we move down and down and down.

The spiritual life calls us down the mountain, into relationship with each other and the earth. The spiritual life calls us down the mountain—rested and restored and ready. And when we get down the mountain, when we land squarely back in the midst of our family and friends, our coworkers and our communities, when we land squarely back in our warring nations and our frightening streets—we need one another more than ever.

Discernment can begin in solitude and in community. Discernment—that process of awareness, intention, truth telling, a willingness to listen, and ultimately, to change—can begin in many ways. An intuitive thought, a hunch, the free flow of conversation, a new idea or creative burst—all of these can initiate the discernment process. We can also welcome discernment with a good night's sleep, a walk in the woods, a time of prayer or meditation, writing or moving or singing, an art class, a concert, a worship service, a rowdy night out with friends, or a circle of committed strangers bent on building whole and healthy lives. But however our bright ideas, our keen intuitions, and our creative bursts emerge, they all must be tested—not only against the reality of the world around us, but also against the pitfalls of ego and self-centeredness and the larger will and good of the world—if they are to attain any level of discernment. This is where both community and solitude come into the picture.

To find and live into our wholeness, we must walk alone and with company, welcoming not only the spiritual practices of solitude but the spiritual practices that call for community as well. But what exactly does a spiritual practice of community look like? There are many forms, of course.

In this culture where so many declare that they are spiritual, but not religious, simply joining a faith community and staying there can be a first step into the spiritual practice of community. Contributing to a greater good beyond ourselves and our own individual needs and wants, learning to trust and even love the sometimes motley crew of humanity that shows up week after week, allowing ourselves to be fed and challenged by diverse teachings and beliefs—all of these experiences and so many more can lead us into the spiritual practice of community.

When I stepped into the Unitarian Society of Northampton and Florence, Massachusetts, at the age of eighteen, I was anything but happy. I had left my home town in Maryland to go away to college —and nearly as soon as my parents pulled away from the curb in the rented minivan, I came out to myself and those around me as a lesbian. I came out, and instead of feeling the rush of relief I had dreamed of, the main thing I felt was fear. Friends at home had been beaten up, sent away, run down by cars, and shamed and disowned by family and friends when they came out, and even though I was miles away, I worried that the same thing would happen to me.

Scared and angry, I did my best to push people away. I got the obligatory flattop coming-out haircut of the time, bought myself a pair of biker boots and a black leather jacket, and suited up in my armor. My anger, and that jacket, became my protection— literally and figuratively. Each morning I'd pull on my boots, run a comb through my one-inch hair, and don the armor of that jacket around me, ready for the assault I was sure the day would bring. To keep myself safe, I put a distance between myself and others, between myself and my vulnerability, as much as possible.

On the outside, I exuded rage. Underneath, I longed for someone to see me. I hoped beyond hope for connection, for wholeness, for relief. I lived in a state of isolation and disconnection. I wrote and prayed—continuing the solitary spiritual practices I learned growing up. But I needed something more.

I walked into Unitarian Universalism frightened and broken, scarred and scattered and angry—not sure if it was safe to hope that this place might be different from all the others, and the community there loved me back together. It happened slowly at first, as I learned to trust again—and then with growing speed, as I let others in. People there welcomed me with open arms, looking me in the eye and extending a hand. They offered me a safe place to come to know myself, inviting me into conversations and leadership opportunities, teaching me to meditate, and including me in small groups for spiritual development. In time, that community and others taught me that I was a valuable, beautiful person, that I had gifts inside me to give, and that I could indeed learn to trust the world again, learning from the pain of the past and making my way forward toward reconciliation and strength. With the church's love then and now, I became whole again, feeling the original blessing we tell one another about when we dedicate our babies, trusting that I could face the world, that I could be in the world, without the armor I held so dear.

I know that not everyone shares my journey, exactly, but I do believe that each of us carries our own scars, our own fears and vulnerability. And I know that, when a community devotes itself to the spiritual practices of welcoming and compassion, amazing things can happen. In community like this we can, as William Blake writes, "learn to endure the beams of love" that surround us, and when we do, we cannot help but shine them on others as well.

Love is not the only gift that the spiritual practice of being in community can bring. New insights, challenges, and deeper commitments can emerge as well.

In our UU Wellspring Spiritual Deepening groups—small groups of committed Unitarian Universalists that join together for a year-long program of spiritual deepening all over the country— each group meeting begins with a reading, silence, and an opportunity for each participant to share about their spiritual practice, their experience with spiritual direction, and anything that is moving in their heart. Each person speaks, uninterrupted, while the group listens. No suggestions or advice are offered. No words of affirmation are spoken. No questions asked. Only attention is given. Attention, and the beams of love from a small circle of fellow travelers, eager to listen and learn from one another.

In one of these groups, a particular participant often struggled with the seemingly insular nature of her life. Each morning began with yoga and meditation, followed by a long day of work and travel. Evenings and weekends meant caring for her aging parents, and she often arrived at our group feeling guilty and frustrated that she wasn't able to do more for the community. "I want to be out there marching," she'd say. "Holding signs and meeting with my elected officials. But I'm too tired. It's all I can do to go to work and pay my bills and care for my parents."

Over the months of our meetings—as each person observed and described the ways that their spiritual practice, and their values, took shape in their lives—this particular participant began to experience a change of heart. Her spiritual practice, she saw, kept her grounded as she cared for her anxious mother and her declining father. Her meditation kept her patient and loving and kind— seeing the pure heart of light and love within her father even as they traveled around and around the same worn carpeted path in the house with his walker, as she offered the endless reassurances and reorientations needed because of his advancing dementia.

By the end of our year together, this participant understood her situation differently. When she moved out from the respite and restoration and insight that her individual spiritual practice offered—when she traveled down the mountain and into the unpredictability and insecurity of the world—she moved directly into caring for her family. And that, it turned out, was her spiritual work of the moment. Through the group's listening and her own speaking, this participant came to a new understanding— an understanding that led to a release of feelings of guilt and an embrace of the challenge at hand: the challenge of caring for her parents with as much kindness and perseverance as she could muster.

No one in the group ever said a word to her to suggest this truth, even though we all saw it. Instead, we listened with rapt attention, shining our beams of love upon her, waiting to see what truth might emerge from within. It was an experience of discernment—both in solitude and in community.

There are times, though, when the difficult but rewarding spiritual work of deep listening—of speaking and hearing without advice or question or challenge—is not all that is called for. Sometimes, asking questions can be a gift of spiritual practice in community, too.

The Quaker author Parker Palmer tells this story in his book, *Let Your Life Speak*:

> [Some time ago] I was offered the opportunity to become the president of a small educational institution. . . . As is the custom in the Quaker community, I called on a half a dozen trusted friends to help me discern my vocation by means of a "clearness committee," a process in which the group refrains from giving you advice but spends three hours asking you honest, open questions to help you discover your own inner truth . . . Halfway into the process, someone asked a question that . . . turned out to be very hard: "What would you like most about being a president?"
>
> The simplicity of the question loosed me from my head and lowered me into my heart. . . . "Well, I would not like having to give up my writing and my teaching . . . I would not like the politics of the presidency, never knowing who your real friends are . . . I would not like having to glad-hand people I do not respect. . . ."
>
> Gently but firmly, the person who had posed the question interrupted me: "May I remind you that I asked what you would most like?"
>
> [Eventually] I felt compelled to give the only honest answer I possessed, an answer that came from the very bottom of my barrel, an answer that appalled even me as I spoke it. "Well . . . I guess what I'd like most is getting my picture in the paper with the word president under it."

Several challenging moments of silence followed, and finally the questioner spoke again, offering another open ended question: "Parker . . . can you think of an easier way to get your picture in the paper?"

Honest, open-ended questions and the time and attention to answer them, surrounded by a circle of love and support—these things only come in community, when we discipline ourselves to ask and to answer, letting go of the assumption that we know what is best for each other.

In this world of increasing isolation for so many, we need one another when it comes to the challenging task of living out our values in our lives. To find and live into our wholeness, we must walk both alone and with company, welcoming in not only the spiritual practices of solitude but also the spiritual practices that call for community. We need one another if we are going to have the strong foundation of love that is required to live with compassion in this world. We need one another if we are to bring our ideas and our serenity down the mountain and into the world, bringing our kindness and compassion to bear in all our relationships, allowing ourselves to change and be changed by all that we encounter. We need one another to listen and to speak and to question. Rev. Mark Morrison-Reed is right: "Alone, our vision is too narrow to see all that must be seen. Together, our vision widens and our strength is renewed."

EXERCISES

Discernment Group

You will need:
- chime or smartphone with a gong application
- timekeeping device

If your group numbers eight or more, gather in groups of four. Otherwise, gather as a whole group. Begin with 5 minutes of silence.

The first person speaks uninterrupted for 15 minutes about "the movement of their life," about Presence as they have experienced it in the previous month, about "interior glances" and what they have revealed, about their spiritual practice in the previous month.

The group sits in silence for a couple minutes before asking some clarifying questions. This is not a support group nor an advice-giving group; the group focuses on the movement of each person's life and their accountabilities to their covenants, promises, and call.

Each person in the group prays out loud for the person who has just spoken. Their language is that of gratitude, blessing, and seeking.

The group sits in silence for 5 minutes before the second person shares. The pattern repeats until each person has spoken.

Close with prayer. This can include prayers for our liberal religious movement and larger political issues of our time. It can simply include prayers that we might be faithful to the One/the Many "Whose We Are."

The group meets monthly.

(This process was originally developed by Rose Mary Dougherty at Shalem Institute and has been adapted for our use.)

Journaling

Write down the ways you notice yourself being teachable this month. What have you learned that has come from an unexpected source?

Resources

One: Whose Am I?

Boorstein, Sylvia. *Happiness Is an Inside Job: Practicing for a Joyful Life*. New York: Ballantine Books, 2008.

Kornfield, Jack. *A Path with Heart: A Guide Through the Perils and Promises of Spiritual Life*. New York: Bantam Books, 1993.

Robinson, Christine, and Alicia Hawkins. *Heart to Heart: Fourteen Gatherings for Reflection and Sharing*. Boston: Skinner House Books, 2009.

Salzburg, Sharon. *LovingKindness: Learning to Love Through Insight Meditation*. Audio CD. Louisville, CO: Sounds True, Inc., 2004.

Two: Who/What Calls Me?

Beach, George Kimmich. *Questions for the Religious Journey: Finding Your Own Path*. Boston: Skinner House Books, 2002.

Palmer, Parker J. *Let Your Life Speak: Listening for the Voice of Vocation*. San Francisco, CA: Jossey-Bass Publishers, 2000.

Two TED talks:

Ford, Justin. *Pedagogy of Privilege*. YouTube, 2012.

McIntosh, Peggy. *How Studying Privilege Systems Can Strengthen Your Compassion*. YouTube, 2012.

Three: Living the Call

Boorstein, Sylvia. *Pay Attention for Goodness' Sake: Practicing the Perfections of the Heart—The Buddhist Path of Kindness.* New York: Random House, 2002.

Goldstein, Joseph, and Jack Kornfield. *Seeking the Heart of Wisdom: The Path of Insight Meditation.* Boston: Shambhala Classics, 1987.

Moffitt, Phillip. *Dancing with Life: Buddhist Insights for Finding Meaning and Joy in the Face of Suffering.* New York: Rodale, 2008.

Muller, Wayne. *Sabbath: Finding Rest, Renewal, and Delight in Our Busy Lives.* New York: Bantam Books, 1999.

Salzberg, Sharon. *Lovingkindness: The Revolutionary Art of Happiness.* Boston: Shambhala, 1997.

Four: Our Covenants

Fowler, James W. *Stages of Faith: The Psychology of Human Development and the Quest for Meaning.* New York: HarperCollins, 1981.

Herz, Walter P., ed. *Redeeming Time: Endowing Your Church with the Power of Covenant.* Boston: Skinner House Books, 1999.

Ogden, Shubert M. *The Reality of God and Other Essays.* Dallas, TX: Southern Methodist University Press, 1992.

Streng, Frederick J. *Understanding Religious Life.* 3rd ed. Boston: Wadsworth Publishing Co., 1984.

Five: Faithfulness

Alexander, Michelle. *The New Jim Crow: Mass Incarceration in the Age of Colorblindness.* New York: The New Press, 2012.

Bennet, Milton J. "Becoming Interculturally Competent" from *Toward Multiculturalism: A Reader in Multicultural Education*. Cambridge, MA: Intercultural Resource Corporation, 2004.

Morrison-Reed, Mark. *Darkening the Doorways: Black Trailblazers and Missed Opportunities in Unitarian Universalism*. Boston: Skinner House Books, 2011.

Wise, Tim. *White Like Me: Reflections on Race from a Privileged Son*. Berkeley, CA: Soft Skull Press, 2008.

Yang, Jeff, ed. *Eastern Standard Time: A Guide to Asian Influence on American Culture from Astro Boy to Zen Buddhism*. Boston: Mariner Books, 1997.

Intercultural Development Inventory. "Developing Intercultural Competence," www.idiinventory.com.

Six: Discernment

Dougherty, Rose Mary. *Group Spiritual Direction: Community for Discernment*. Mahwah, NJ: Paulist Press, 1995.

Palmer, Parker J. The Center for Courage and Renewal.π www.couragerenewal.org

———. *A Hidden Wholeness: The Journey Toward an Undivided Life*. San Francisco, CA: John Wiley & Sons, Inc, 2004.

Wolff, Pierre. *Discernment: The Art of Choosing Well*. Liguori, MO: Liguori/Triumph, 1993.

About the Contributors

Jen Crow is the minister of program life at the First Universalist Church in Minneapolis, Minnesota. She has also served as associate minister of the First Unitarian Church in Rochester, New York. She draws particular inspiration from our Universalist and Transcendentalist ancestors, and is the founder of Wellspring, a Unitarian Universalist program of spiritual deepening (www.uuwellspring.com).

Lisa Jennings is a professor and the director of vascular biology in the Department of Internal Medicine at the University of Tennessee Health Science Center and is a biotechnology entrepreneur. She has been a member of the First Unitarian Church of Memphis since 1983 and has served as president of the board of trustees there. She has also served as president of the Unitarian Universalist Southwestern Conference.

Sarah Lammert is the director of ministries and faith development at the Unitarian Universalist Association. She also serves as the UUA's ecclesiastical endorser, and particularly enjoys working with Unitarian Universalist military chaplains. She has served as minister of the Unitarian Universalist Church of Ogden, Utah, and the Unitarian Society of Ridgewood, New Jersey. She practices lovingkindness meditation daily.

Bret Lortie is the senior minister of the Unitarian Church of Evanston, Illinois. He also serves the Civil Air Patrol, both as a chaplain and as a search and rescue pilot. He has served as minister of the Unitarian Universalist Church of San Antonio, Texas.

Jon Luopa is the senior minister of University Unitarian Congregation in Seattle, Washington. He has served as minister of the Unitarian Society of Hartford, Connecticut, and First Parish in Hingham, Massachusetts. He teaches the Unitarian Universalist polity and history courses at Seattle University's School of Theology and Ministry.

Suzelle Lynch is the minister of Unitarian Universalist Church West, in Brookfield, Wisconsin. She also served as minister of the Kitsap Unitarian Universalist Fellowship in Bremerton, Washington, and was one of the first members of the Unitarian Universalist Ministers Association's Committee on Ministry for Antiracism, Anti-oppression, and Multiculturalism.

William G. Sinkford is the senior minister of the First Unitarian Church in Portland, Oregon. He has served as the president of the Unitarian Universalist Association and as director of congregational district extension services there.

Susan M. Smith is a congregational life consultant for the Southern Region of the Unitarian Universalist Association, focusing on leadership training and content curation. She has served as the emerging congregation consultant for the Florida and Michigan Districts and as minister of the First Universalist Unitarian Church of East Liberty, Michigan.

Don Southworth is the executive director of the Unitarian Universalist Ministers Association. He has served as minister of the Eno River Unitarian Universalist Fellowship in Durham, North Carolina, the Northwest Unitarian Universalist Congregation in Atlanta, Georgia, and the First Unitarian Universalist Society of San Francisco. He worked in the corporate world for twenty years and has a passion for the intersection between entrepreneurship and spirituality, or "calltrepreneurship" as he names it.

Douglas Taylor is the minister of the Unitarian Universalist Church in Binghamton, New York. He has served as associate minister of the Cedar Lane Unitarian Universalist Church in Bethesda, Maryland. He is a fourth-generation Universalist and is the son of a Unitarian Universalist minister.

Cheryl M. Walker is the minister of the Unitarian Universalist Fellowship of Wilmington, North Carolina. She has also served as assistant minister of the Unitarian Church of All Souls in New York City.

Jenny Weil works as a consultant to churches and nonprofits and currently serves on the Board of Trustees of the Starr King School for the Ministry. She has been a member of the First Unitarian Church of Dallas, Texas, since 2003.